GW00692276

Pages From A Medium's Diary

By Shirley Willcox

First published in Great Britain in 2009
by
Shirley Willcox

Copyright © 2009 Shirley Willcox

Names, characters and related indicia are copyright and trademark
Copyright © 2009 Shirley Willcox

Shirley Willcox has asserted her moral rights
to be identified as the author

All rights reserved; no part of this publication may be reproduced or
transmitted by any means, electronic, mechanical, photocopying or
otherwise without the written permission of the publisher.

Cover designed by
Adam Carruthers, Hill Street, Wisbech

Printed in Great Britain
by the MPG Books Group,
Bodmin and King's Lynn

About The Author And Book

Τhis book is a diary of readings I have given to people covering over 60 years.

When a person comes to my home it is often to seek assurance that someone who has died, who they were close to and loved, is safe in the spirit world.

I cannot contact a spirit, but usually the loved one sought will make contact with me, show him or her self, and give advice, love and messages, for me to pass on.

Each chapter of my book is a reading given by me in private or at a public function.

There has often been a follow up that covers years.

Often these chapters are sad, even brutal, but I've told it as it is, in truth.

I have made many friends in the sitters I have met, and hope I've brought comfort and love from their departed.

Shirley Willcox

Names have been changed to protect people's identities

Dedications

This book is dedicated to:

Victoria Barrett
My young granddaughter who is in New Zealand

Gemma Baker (actress)
My young friend and helper

Acknowledgements

I would like to thank Roxanne for being my taxi on all my missions, and for always being there to help me.

Thank you, Dominique: you always came to my Evenings of Clairvoyance, and supported me at the Spiritualist Church services.

Victoria my granddaughter for always listening and believing in me; thank you it meant so much.

Bill my son-in-law for always providing help at the time it is needed. Thank you for your support.

My husband and the rest of my family.

Gemma, thank you for giving me the nudge to start the book, and for your help.

Jean Harmon for her dedication to find and get justice for her son Jimmy

I would like to pay a tribute to Graham Punter (Late) who worked for the Citizen newspaper in Wisbech: a thorough gentleman who listened, was kind and wrote the truth about Jimmy Harmon's murder. We owe him our gratitude and thanks.

Preface

Have you ever stopped and noticed the leaves of a daffodil on a cold December day, when the earth is frozen hard with snow or frost? How does the delicate leaf push through? We find the earth too hard for a spade or fork. It is one of life's miracles. The seasons, nature, we take it all for granted.

What goes on out there? If a daffodil can come back to life, is it any different from us and re-birth?

Why do some folk live until they are 90 years old and others go at 19 years? I truly think our lives are mapped out at birth and we are taken at God's will.

A medium is a person who sees spirit, a clairvoyant hears spirit, and a fortune teller can give accurate predictions for the future.

I hope I have helped the many thousands of people I've seen, at evenings of clairvoyance, services in Spiritualist churches, fetes and private sittings. Many, many have returned to me and confirmed the predictions as accurate. Married the name I've given them, dates of births, deaths, children born, countries visited; it must all run into the thousands.

I haven't written the private, secret sittings, or named the famous and well-known sitters I have had come to see me. But I have met an enormous amount of caring, wonderful people who have enriched my life by allowing me to participate in theirs.

I think we are all born with "Special Gifts" and I will be forever grateful for the wonderful gift given to me. Being a medium has helped me provide answers to many questions, but it often still astounds me quite how it all works.

How did an old Red Indian Chief materialise to me in my own home? He had a full head of distinctive feathers, his eyes were so bright, and the whites glistened. His face was weathered brown with harsh lines around his mouth and forehead. He was so close and solid I could have touched his leathered skin. He looked right at me! It was as though he was alive. He did not say one word – he lingered, and then he was gone. I felt humbled and proud that such a spirit had visited me. This is the most rewarding presence I've ever been in and will remember it until the day I die.

Introduction

I am the seventh of ten children born in Ilford, Essex, and spent most of my life there.

The family, with ten children, naturally was poor. We did not have holidays; just the odd day to Southend or Brighton. However, the very best holiday of my young life was when we were evacuated all as a family to Burnage, Manchester. I will always remember it as an adventure, and we were very lucky we survived the London blitz; yes, I remember it very well.

There was a shelter at the bottom of the garden where we slept most nights curled up on bunks. All the doors and windows of all the houses were blown off, and I remember glass and rubble every where. Every one seemed kind and looked out for each other.

All fruit (apples pears cherries etc.) were stripped from the trees and shared; always there would be a cabbage, some potatoes, vegetables of all sorts and fruit left on our doorstep.

If only people were like this now - how many times have we noticed fruit rotting on trees.

Our local park was all turned into vegetable plots and

lots of Italian prisoners of war worked the fields.

The prisoners were very kind to us; obviously they missed their wives and families, and never did a day go by when they would send us home without produce. I was seven or eight years old, all of my brothers and sisters were one year apart and, being children and innocent, they found us amusing and treated us fondly.

School was not a problem: we did not go! Teachers were never there; if the air raid went off, we were told to run home, but we all used to gang up in the park. Shrapnel rained from the sky, doodle bugs screamed overhead, and jerry planes were all over the skies.

The area where we lived was very close to a massive ammunition factory - only five minutes from our home, in fact. Black-out was highest on the agenda because every man woman and child knew of the consequences of a hit on Plessey's.

I was nine when the war was over, and we all adjusted to our lives. By now I was seeing spirits regularly; occasionally I would tell things and more than once got a bash around the head as my mother did not like what I was saying. I was I suppose, an odd little girl off in my own world but I saw things, and I knew things.

I did quite well at school considering the lack of attendance; I passed the eleven plus for high school but was not allowed to go because the fares and uniform were too expensive.

I turned up at the local secondary school for the start of term, but they had not got a place for me as I was not expected. However my sister, who was one year older, attended and I was allowed to stay.

I did remarkably well; I'm very proud to say, I was top of the class. I won swimming cups, sports cups and excelled at art, but at fourteen years I had to leave school and get a job to contribute to the household.

My work experience was not an exciting part of my life. I look back on those years as existing. I spent several years working in a butchers shop; not the sort of job for a young girl – but it was found for me and I was trained to be grateful.

I married the boy I had known since I was about four or five years, old who lived around the corner. Like all married people, we worked, we struggled, we raised our children.

My personal life is private but I am lucky enough to have three happily married children and eight wonderful grandchildren. Peter and I have weathered almost fifty years and we live in a beautiful beamed cottage with enough room to have all the family here.

Contents

1
War and Gypsies

I was born in 1936. When the war ended I was 9 years old. The world had changed. There was a massive gathering in our local Valentines Park for VE day. Enormous crowds descended, bonfires were everywhere. This had all been denied for so long because of the black outs. Bright sparkling fireworks screamed overhead. It was thrilling; probably my first ever sighting of a firework. Everyone was kissing, hugging, loud brass bands were playing all the much loved tunes: 'We'll Meet Again', 'White cliffs of Dover', and we all sang our hearts out. As dusk descended, thousands of uniformed men and women were dancing on the green. Yes, the war was finally over.

The fun fairs began to fill the field. Hundreds of caravans appeared in our park and open fields, along with lorries, merry go rounds, boat swings, dodgems and side shows. The excitement was unbelievable. We'd never seen anything like it before. During day time children could ride for free. The owners said they wanted to bring the fun fair back to life and what better way than through children's laughter. It was a god-send to us as no one had any money.

As a family we spent our school holidays let loose in the

park. No adult, no supervision; one of us had a pack of jam sandwiches to share and there were lots of drinking fountains scattered around.

I liked to go off alone. I didn't always want to go fishing in the brooks, help out at the boat yard with my brothers to get a free boat ride, or even go scrumping in the orchard. I liked to hang around caravans. My favourites were the old fashioned round-top ones that were drawn by horses.

I'd sit on the step of my chosen van, which was with all the others, horses grazing nearby. One day there was a half door open; today we would call it a stable door. A dark haired lady in bright silk clothes was cooking at the stove.

"Hello", she said, "I've seen you before. Haven't you got any friends?" she asked.

If only she knew. I liked to escape sometimes, just to be myself. I came from a very large family and it was nice to be alone, not taken for granted, not be made to do or go along with what others wanted.

"I just like the caravans", I answered.

A younger girl then arrived; she had a very fat tummy and, young as I was, we all knew about babies.

"Your little boy died. His lungs couldn't work properly", I told her. "But that baby in your belly is a girl",

"Mum!" the girl screamed, "what have you told this kid?"

The older lady who had spoken to me earlier had witnessed what I had said.

"Would you like to come in here dear?" she indicated to the caravan.

"Yes, I'd love to", I leapt up the steps, barging through the door.

The young pregnant lady was sitting by a small table. On it was a large crystal ball. My brothers had large marbles and I'd always pinched them so I could see things, but they were not nearly as big as this one. I'd moved over to the large crystal ball sitting on a stand on a velvet cloth.

"Tell us about the baby boy", the older woman asked me.

"He's on your shoulder. He has golden hair and it's pretty, it curls. His name is Reuben", I was pointing at the young lady. She started to cry.

Looking back, this was probably the first time I'd given a reading to a stranger. I was still only nine years old.

They offered me some of their stew. It was delicious.

I was allowed to look in the crystal ball and saw a number 7.

"Your baby will come on the 7th and she will be lovely", I told them.

"I'd like one of her names to be yours", the young girl said. They didn't even know my name at this point, so it was a bit of a gamble on their part, but I was thrilled.

The baby arrived on the 7th, and it was a little girl. I was invited to hold her. She was gorgeous and fair haired like her brother.

I often had a meal with the gypsies. I always went alone; it was my very own secret. I met lots of their relatives, and was often asked to look into the crystal ball and tell them what I saw. They were very kind to me, and there is a very big place for them in my heart.

Since my move to Cambridge I have met many more gypsies. I always think it strange that they come to see me. I didn't realise they do not communicate with spirits because they believe they are disturbing the dead. I respect them. They are good people and I admire the way the families look out for each other.

2

Carlton Leach

The phone shrilled out loud. This was nothing new, as the phone never stopped in my house.

"Hello can I help you?"

A young man. "Are you Shirley?"

"Yes"

"The clairvoyant?"

"Yes"

"Did you live in Otley Drive, Gant's Hill?"

"Yes"

"Are you elderly? – You don't sound it"

"Yes "– then I laughed, so many questions

Again, "how can I help you "

He started to babble – he desperately wanted to see me soon.

I looked in my diary, squeezed in an appointment, and then he said he couldn't make it by ten o clock

"Oh what sort of time is ok for you" I asked?

"Well, the journey will take me at least three and a half hours"

"No I said, don't bother to come here; there are lots of mediums around, find someone local"

"No" he said "it must be you – I'll tell you when I see you"

Now intrigued, I gave him a Saturday morning appointment

Not usual as I like my family to stay at weekends, and I'm almost retired.

The boy arrived and I soon got into his life. I told him all sorts but nothing remarkable to have made him make the very long journey.

I was a little uneasy; was I a disappointment to him? Had I not got the message he so desperately wanted?

"I had to ask, why did you have to see me?"

"It's the book - the one you're in. I was so impressed I searched every where for you and out of the blue my sister said she knew you, and had visited you at Gant's Hill, and two months ago she came to Cambridge to see you"

I can understand why he had difficulty finding me; I have never advertised in my life. I feel if people are meant to see me, they will find me.

"What book?" I said. "I don't understand He told me he had read ' Muscle' by Carlton Leach, a book about the Essex Boys and the Rettendon murders.

A whole chapter was about me!

I wasn't familiar with the name Carlton Leach. Everyone comes to me anonymously; that is the way I like it. However, the Rettendon murders, I *was* familiar with.

After the young man had left, happy with my predictions and all I had told him, my determination was to find the book and read it.

The local library, Smiths, Waterstones, etc.did not have it, so I ordered it from the library. It always takes ages when you desperately want something! Finally the card came, my book was in and waiting for collection. Perhaps through vanity I scanned it for the chapter about me.

I was spellbound - it was written with great sensitivity, with none of the knocks or ridicule normally directed at psychics. I was moved and enormously proud that I had been written about.

I won't bore you with all the facts, but reading about the time I had spent with Carlton Leach has made me want to complete the clairvoyance side of the evidence we can pass on to the public.

I haven't met up with Mr. Leach since his sitting with me but I value the time I spent with him and thank him for inspiring me to write.

3
David

One sunny afternoon, two sisters came to my home. I told them several things, but a presence was dominant. He said his name was David I felt a terrible pain at the back of my head. I saw a white van. I felt I was being pushed and kicked out onto the road. Murder was coming to my mind and I told the girls. I pick up the pain and symptoms when a spirit is with me.

The pain in my head killed David There was not a lot of response from the girls, but they wanted me to tell them more.

I described what I could see.

"He is showing me a pub, with an orange tree or blossom. It's a large building with a lower roof to the right side, a winding path with railings and small concrete posts and a pond to the right side of the path. One of the concrete posts has fallen",

I drew a picture.

The sisters were intrigued. They said he died in a hit and run accident.

"No. It was murder" I told them. I also told them other personal things, and then they went.

A few weeks later I got a phone call - it was a News of The World reporter. Then the television programme "The Cook Report" called; could they come and see me?

"When?" I asked.

"Now - we're outside your house."

The interview was intriguing. They fired questions at me non-stop and I was shocked to be shown a tracing of a pub and grounds exactly like the drawing of the Orange Tree pub I had drawn for the two sisters of murdered David. There was even a fallen post exactly as in my drawing.

"We would like to take you to this pub and area and for you to tell us what you pick up."

All was arranged for two days later. They would collect me at 8am and see what the day brought.

We set off in a lovely, posh car. The journey took us to Middlesex where we met up with the two sisters and mother of David

We started our day at the Orange Tree pub. I felt odd and restless. We passed the fallen concrete post and all was there just as I had seen in my vision at my home. Immediately I went to the small public bar area. He was there! David's spirit was with me, and I suddenly felt agitated. I hurried from the pub followed closely by the others. Then I started to run, I didn't know where; the area was completely unknown to me. I passed a couple of turnings, stopped and burst into tears.

"He was here in his car and dragged out of it", I said shaking. Everyone was stunned. They were all looking at me in shock. I did not know, but this was the very spot his Porsche car was found. I was crying and shaking and started to run again. Everyone chased after me again - poor lot! We were on a very busy, long 'A' road. I kept hurrying then stopped.

"He is here!" I stood standing still in the road. Unbeknown to me the body was found in this exact spot. I saw David being booted out the back of a van. To our right was a sloped bank with lots of bushes. I saw a gap in the bushes and hurried to the spot. It looked down on the road, a clear view of the death scene, and there at my feet were a set of keys. Unbeknown to me David's car keys were missing and provided vital evidence to the enquiry. These were the keys. The inquiry changed to murder, not hit and run.

Later that day the spirit of David took me to his best friend's house. I stopped outside a house and said I felt very safe and wanted to go in. The family told me it was where David spent his childhood.

Still driving around the area I pleaded with the driver to stop the car. This time I walked up a path and stroked the door. David's family told me it was the first house David had bought when he got married.

On another occasion to assist the inquiry we all went to Elstree Airport, and out of 100's of planes I picked out the one David had used.

I was glad to be of help to this case. Clairvoyants do have a very exciting life.

4
Kevin

Children are very spiritual. They are totally innocent and just accept what they see. My work often involves children, like when a group of us organised an evening of clairvoyance to raise money for a little boy named Kevin.

His grandmother had come to my house and in the reading I told her:

"The spirits are showing me a little boy. He's blonde haired, blue eyed, gorgeous. But the spirits are concerned about his health. I'm afraid they are showing me a wheel chair, and I think he'll have to change schools",

"Actually", the grandmother said, "you're right Shirley. My grandson, that's him you've just described. He's in a wheelchair. He was born with a genetic defect. When he was about 18months old he got sick and that's when this defect was picked up. He'll be in a wheelchair for the rest of his life",

I saw and got to know Kevin over many years and grew very fond of him and his family.

His family asked me one day whether I had seen an item on the television about a policeman who had been shot.

This policeman had been confined to a wheelchair, but had got a new device that enabled some wheelchair users to get up and walk unassisted. The family needed £4000 to buy this device. I didn't need to be asked twice to help out. Immediately I got in touch with other mediums, I booked a hall, and got some tickets printed.

The evening was a wonderful success. Lots of people came and lots of mediums gave private readings. The money was raised and Kevin was able to buy his walking frame.

Two girls arrived at my house. They were rather subdued and very young, about 17 and 18 I think. They were dressed very fashionably with big, clanging earrings, mini skirts and long boots.

We went upstairs and we all sat down. It surprised me that they didn't sit closely together there was a very large space between them.

Then the very first thing I saw was a white gown and it was making a rustling noise.

I kept asking them,

"Can you hear that, the rustling noise?"

"No, we can't", they both replied.

Suddenly between the two girls stood an angelic looking man. He was about 6'6 tall and had massive angel wings. The light was so bright that it was dazzling me. All I can say is he looked like an Adonis. The two girls were puzzled by me as if I was mad, and all I could do was gasp.

"Kevin, Kevin, Kevin", I kept saying.

The girls began to cry.

"Are you alright?" I asked them.

"You know him, you know him. He's only died just now. He died half an hour before we left home. You know our Nan, and you've known him for years", one of the girls cried.

I looked again. Of course! This was Kevin, the young boy in the wheelchair. He was 16 now. I had only ever seen him doubled up in his chair, but standing tall he had transfigured into a beautiful angel. He had evolved within a few minutes of passing. He had served his penance on earth and stepped into another realm as this wonderful angel.

It was one of the most amazing things I have ever seen. These two girls when they arrived were so ordinary, I didn't imagine experiencing this kind of phenomena when they walked through the door.

"I can't take all this in", I said, overwhelmed by it all.

"Ann, our Nan has got to come and see you Shirley. She's in bits", the girls exclaimed.

"Of course please tell her to come whenever she wants",

"We didn't know whether to come. We don't want a reading for ourselves, but our Nan said to come along as you might see Kevin", the girls said.

"You must go home and tell her what you have heard", I told them.

"I feel different in this room", one of the girls said.

"Yeah, me too", the other agreed.

They had both finally stopped crying. Then suddenly the room was filled with the fragrance of flowers. I can't understand how this happened, but I could smell freesias and sweet pea, one of the girls smelt lavender, the other could smell roses. It was as though the whole room was filled with the perfume of flowers.

Kevin left. It was magical and mind-blowing.

We decided to go downstairs for a cup of tea and a chat as the girls said they felt a bit spooked. They had a car parked outside but felt too wobbly to drive. Whilst they smoked I made them a ham sandwich and more tea.

I said to them, "You know, seeing him standing so tall, standing proud, could any of us wish him to be doubled up in a wheel chair? It's like he's free at last",

Kevin leaving would leave an enormous hole in many lives, undoubtedly his mum and dad, but also his Nan. They were so close. But this boy had a sweet nature and character for all to see when he was on earth, and in spirit. I saw an angel in Kevin.

When the girls left they immediately went round to tell their Nan what had happened. I got a phone call shortly afterwards. It was Ann.

"Shirley, please can I see you?" she cried.

"Yes of course you can. Come round", I told her.

She arrived with her husband, but said he would stay downstairs as he wanted Ann to have the reading to herself as Kevin was her life. We went upstairs.

I was picking up something.

"Please don't be afraid but I can see a picture wiggling off the wall. I'm seeing a picture of Kevin. It's hung on the wall at your house. He's going to move it. It's going to spin around then come off the wall", I said.

We chatted for ages then she left.

The next day the whole family gathered around Ann's

house to plan the funeral. They were all sitting in the living room when all of a sudden there was a clanking noise on the wall. They all turned to look as Kevin's picture swung on the wall where it hung, then it landed smack on the other side of the room on the table spinning. It didn't break.

The whole family were witness to something quite amazing and I am sure it gave them comfort to know Kevin was still there, ever present.

5

Paul (Adult cot death)

B elgravia in London is home to a very well known psychic centre. It is a very famous building belonging to the psychic movement.

A friend told me Doris Stokes was going to be there and, along with Paul's parents (the young man who had died in the plane crash),we decided we would go along to the seminar next Saturday.

When we arrived it was packed, but we were very lucky. We were in the second row and Doris Stokes was sitting just a couple of yards away from us. She smiled and chatted. She was a very friendly person, but she wasn't feeling very well that day.

The seminar was very enjoyable and relaxed. It focused on how mediums worked, how they began, how they took services at spiritualist churches and insights into Doris Stokes' life. It wasn't intimidating or too "way-out"; everyone was talking to each other and it was extremely friendly.

There was a lady and a gentleman sitting in front of me. She was tiny and he was very large. A spirit boy was hovering between them. He took my attention. I had come along to see Doris Stokes, but this boy was so prominent. He kept looking into the face of this lady and gentleman, his mother and father, then looking straight at me. He was wafting between the pair of them.

"Please talk to her, please talk to her", he said to me, referring to his mother.

I knew I'd like to talk to her, but I thought it best I wait until we had our tea break. That came about 5 minutes later and the lady and her husband wondered over to us three and we all started chatting. This was my cue to tell her what I had seen.

"You do know you have a tall, very handsome young man in spirit with you? He's got beautiful brown hair, big brown eyes and a lovely smile",

Both of them gazed at each other, their eyes filled with tears. I continued.

"He's telling me his name's Paul. He's very safe and he's at peace",

I don't like telling people things under these sorts of circumstances. It can look like you're showing off, so I suggested if they would like to come to my home instead for a proper reading. The lady took my phone number and we continued with the seminar which was thoroughly enjoyable.

Quite a few months later I got a telephone call out of the blue from the lady at the seminar.

"Shirley, I've heard quite a lot about you since I met you. When I got home I phoned my cousin to ask if she knew you, she lives in Gants Hill too. She said 'Yes I know Shirley, she does evenings of clairvoyance and loads of people go to her for readings'. I said 'Is she alright? It was a little strange the way she just blurted out things about Paul.' My cousin explained that it was how mediums worked- you see a spirit and just say what you see. I've never been to see a medium before. I was only at the Doris Stoke's seminar out of curiosity",

We made an arrangement for her to come and visit. She was going to bring her husband and a young girl.

They came to my house and I was struck by how stunningly beautiful the young girl was. She was dainty, graceful, an incredible beauty.

"You've got to be Paul's fiancée", I said.

"Yes", she said looking very distant, sad and obviously very tearful.

"Paul left this earth very suddenly. It's almost as if he fell asleep",

"That's exactly how it happened", all three said.

Paul had died from adult cot death. He was a perfectly fit young man who had been out playing football and then come home. Paul and his fiancée were due to be married in a couple of months with a very large, expensive wedding planned.

Caroline, Paul's fiancée phoned him the next day and there was no answer. She went round to the house, the curtains were drawn, and it all seemed terribly quiet. He had gone to bed and not woken up.

It was all so sad. He had the world at his feet.

Without thinking, as it so often happens, I said,

"Caroline, Paul is telling me you will marry a doctor and

have two children. He says 'We were never meant to be.'"

She screamed at me, "How dare you say that? I don't want to hear this! I love Paul. I will never marry anyone else. How can you say this?"

"But it isn't me saying this, I'm just repeating what Paul is telling me", I explained. I sympathised; what I had said was a lot to take in, insensitive even, but felt obliged to repeat what Paul was saying.

After that visit Paul's parents continued to visit me over the years and his sister too. Caroline eventually did marry a doctor and had two children. I often wonder why these young souls are taken. I can only believe God needs them in the spirit world.

6

"Herald of Free Enterprise"

Two young boys approx 17 years old came to see me in London. They were hardly seated when a girl of seventeen came through - she said her name was Jenny and put her hands out to one of the lads. "

Steve, Steve you have lovely blue eyes",

"Oh my god" they both said.

"She was always saying that, this is so weird, I did not know you could know things like this", Steve said

"The scene's changed; there is lots of water, it's very cold, there's a massive boat and lots of people in the water. It's horrible - people are screaming and drowning; a complete disaster!" I told them

"This was March 6ᵗʰ or 7ᵗʰ - The Herald of Free Enterprise, Zeebrugge" I was saying. "Hold on - a dreadful disaster"

Steve and Jenny plus two friends spent the day on this boat. When the boat toppled over the four friends fell from an enormous height. Jenny struck her head on an object, Steve held her head above water for nine hours; he thought she was unconscious – she was dead.

They were only youngsters but Jenny's death totally traumatized Steve, to the point of nearly having a complete nervous breakdown.

Steve was not invited to go to the funeral, and he was so grief-stricken he lost the plot. He got in his car and drove and drove and ended up in Scotland. He was stopped by the police and was so distraught he couldn't talk. The police put him in a cell for the night and it was only when his parents had the car traced that he was released, numb with shock.

Life can be so cruel. Steve wrote to me several times, and sent me a photo of Jenny. I still have her photo on my wall and one of his letters. This sort of disaster can often leave the survivor in a sad state of limbo, often questioning why they survived when others died, especially the adored, cherished girlfriend. Jenny still visits me as a sort of 'chaperone' to souls who have newly passed, who want to make contact with loved ones on the earth plane. If ever Jenny's spirit appears, while I'm with a sitter, I know a loved relative or friend has tragically drowned or died in similar circumstances to her, in water.

Jenny is still a young, beautiful soul, another precious child chosen to go at a very young age.

7

Terry Venables

Every now and again I was asked to give an evening of clairvoyance. Lots of people who wanted information about psychics and spirits could not attend spiritualist churches during the daytime because of work commitments, and it did not take a lot of organization.

I knew lots of folks who would print and sell tickets, and also serve and contribute half time refreshments. Old favourites like home- made bread pudding and home- made flap jacks, tea, coffee or fruit juice given with kindness - my psychic friends were always willing to help.

The Lambourne Room (the lower ball room at the Ilford Town Hall) was a favourite venue, with easy access to buses, trains and parking. It also had excellent kitchens and cloakrooms.

Tickets sales were rapid; this time the charity by popular choice was the kidney and renal department at Great Ormond Street hospital.

Two mediums were taking the platform: a friend and I would give three hours between us of clairvoyance to the eager audience.

I struck lucky with one of the visitors to my house, as

Mrs. Christine Venables arrived for a private reading. I happened to mention her mother's kidney trouble, and it seemed she was having spirit healing and making wonderful progress. I mentioned the evening of clairvoyance we were doing and she immediately offered a football signed by her husband's Barcelona football team (Terry Venables being the club manager). It would be our star raffle prize.

The whole evening was a wonderful success.

At the end of the evening a pretty young blonde girl came over to see me. I had given her a message but she couldn't or wouldn't accept it. I felt a little embarrassed up there reeling various things about a boy named Billy - yes she admitted she knew him, also had him as her best man, former boyfriend, and childhood sweetheart, but she kept saying "no, no, no", to each message – the last being he died from a terrible fall.

"Shirley, he committed suicide, he was on drugs, recovering from a mental break down, and had dabbled with the occult",

"My husband became so jealous of him I used to cut our talks short",

"When he died I felt so guilty I rowed and rowed with my husband",

"I thought it was because I pushed him out of my life",

"He had fallen from an enormous height, when you said he sends love to us all, and thank you for naming my little son after him, I was so happy I was crying inside - this means he has forgiven us",

"Please don't blame yourself for his death, dear" I said,

"If someone is hell bent on doing it, no one will stop them",

I was so pleased; she had told me it was so draining giving message after message for someone to blank you. I was now very tired but it was now worth it, a very rewarding evening. A very large cheque was ready to be handed over to the hospital, and I decided to deliver it personally. The doctor in the renal unit invited me to see his tiny patients attached to the dialysis machines and equipment you can only wonder at.

Our efforts were going to such a good cause, and we received a wonderful thank-you letter which I copied and sent to everyone that had contributed to the successful evening.

I have to this day the letter, dated 21/ 1 /1987 and it is very faded.

8
Jimmy

It was a cold winter evening, a Thursday. Three ladies were at my door. I immediately felt drawn to the two younger ladies. The older lady I kindly asked not to come in. She was furious.

"I'm not going. This concerns all of us",

I stood my ground.

"I'm sorry, it's just not right for the 3 of you together", I apologised and the older lady agreed to leave after I said I would see her individually next week.

The two other ladies and I went up to my little room. I felt the girls were bonded. I told them various things and knew one had a son and the other a daughter. Their children's father was the same; both girls linked in this way. The room was freezing. Yes, it was mid-winter but my heating was working okay. This was the spirit making the room icy cold.

"There's a young man here. He has only just passed to spirit. It's horrible. He is afraid, scared, lost and it's very black. You are both bonded to him but, I'm so sorry, you will never see him alive again. You both know he is missing

The children's dad- it was him!

"He has been murdered. Garrotted", I was spooked. One girl started to cry and question me. The other just sat, numb. We were all in shock.

"You are sure?" One of the girls asked me.

"Yes. His name is Jimmy", I was tearful and shocked too. I felt awful, but I just open my mouth and information comes out.

The girls left, leaving me feeling uneasy, but this was not an everyday session.

Five ladies arrived promptly for their sitting. We were all sitting quietly, I was waiting and tuning to the spirit world.

The room was freezing; a presence was definitely here. I usually go round the room, working from the right first, but I was immediately drawn to the lady in the middle.

"Jimmy is here. He's calling you 'Mum'. He is in the dark and it's muddy. There is only a head! He is scared", I suddenly knew this spirit had been to see me before- the two girls with the two children.

This was awful. A murder. The mother was distraught.

"He is missing. He will come back", she said.

I had already told the girls he was dead, I couldn't lie to the mother.

"I'm so sorry. He has gone", I said as gently as I could.

"NO! NO! You can't mean this!"

A vision was with me. There were three men with him outside a house, he was being dragged and supported, and he looked terrible. "Barking Creek" was being given to me as the area where it happened. I felt a severe blow to the kidney area in the back, and a tightening around the throat.

The atmosphere in the room was electric.

"What are they doing to my son? Who are they?" the mother called out.

I was giving names and details and it was morbid. No calm, no peace, just total turmoil. What had I seen? It was too terrible to take in. The poor mother was left deeply shaken and upset and they left.

On Dec 14th 1999 I moved from my home of 40 years in Otley Drive, Gants Hill Essex to a tiny village in Cambridgshire. My husband retired after some 50 years in the building trade. Not many folk knew of our escape to the country. I had always taken appointments anonymously and had never advertised. People always found me through word of mouth.

Our new home needed updating and we both happily spent hours each day painting and generally improving the place. My time was spent doing and making a lovely front garden. The area is enormous so I set out rockeries and flower beds and planted lots of climbing ivies to hide the ugly walls. I added hanging baskets, two lampposts, a wishing well with a pump and a small pond full of frogs.

The interior is pretty and complements the quaint character of the cottage, but with a builder as a husband I can't claim the honour of refurbishment. All of this DIY of course put clairvoyance out of the picture, but gradually people were beginning to find me and track me down.

One day the phone went.

"Shirley, do you remember me? It's Jean, Jimmy's mum",

"Oh yes! I do!" After the traumatic sitting in my old

home was I ever to forget her?

"Jimmy is still missing. Nobody has seen him or found anything", I wanted to stay quiet. This lady could not comprehend he was gone. "Please help me. I don't know about mediums or spirits, but I did like you",

I have over the years done lots of spirit readings on the phone. Whilst talking to Jean I hoped her loved ones other than Jimmy would come through. Jean's husband started to come through to me. He told me the way he'd passed. I repeated everything I heard word for word, a lung removed. Cancer. He said the name "Elvin

"Is that correct? I've never heard that name before",

"Oh yes", said Jean. Then a lady called Annie was there, and another lady who said she was "Nanny Cardigan" and was looking after Jimmy.

Jean was very grateful. All these people were family and it was helping her come to terms with her missing son.

Jean phoned me often as she came to the realisation Jimmy was gone. We laughed, we cried and we often asked why.

In September 2000 Jean asked me if I would go out with the police to search for Jimmy. I did not have an exact location to find him, but knew it was the Barking Creek area and was prepared to go and see if I could help.

A police officer collected me from my daughter's house as we were staying down in the Gants Hill area. We went out, but it was not a success. He was scared and agitated in my company, and I was on edge.

He took me to a place at Barking Creek, but it was all wrong. I felt I was on the wrong side of the river. I needed to be near grass, not on a concrete harbour. I wanted to leave. I did not feel comfortable with someone who was scared of me.

We drove off, but suddenly I was happy.

"Please drive down this turning. Turn right and then the second right", I instructed him. Jimmy's spirit was here. He took me to a house, number 17. "Please stop", I asked. A vision came to me. I saw three men dragging Jimmy from the front door; he was barely alive and very poorly. I had seen this before in my home when his mum was there. It was odd. I felt ill. Something was definitely here.

Suddenly the policeman received an urgent emergency phone call. He dumped me in the middle of Ilford and drove off like the wind. I was disgusted; I felt used and furious. It was hot, stuffy, crowded and I was crying. Then I realised - what an idiot- it wasn't rejection or feeling used by the police that had upset me; it was Jimmy's spirit coming through me, within me. This makes mediums cry, however tough we might think we are.

I went back to my daughter's house, hugged my gorgeous grandson and vowed never to go out with the police again.

Later that day Jean phoned me.

"Shirley you must go out with the police again. The top detective wants to meet you",

"No way I'm not interested", I couldn't face another trip with a cynical officer of the law.

"But you must! He believes in mediums. I've given him your phone number",

"Great. Thank you", I said sarcastically.

The detective phoned me.

"I would like you to accompany me on a police search of the River Thames near Barking Creek for Jimmy Harmon's body",

"No. I am just not interested. And anyway, his body is not out mid-river. He is near a grid in still water and mud He argued about the search, but I did not intend spending another day being ridiculed by "The Law I repeated, "No way, not interested

"Why not come for the day out? You could boast to your friends that you'd spent the day on a police launch I put the phone down on him.

Jean was upset. She thought I'd left her and was no longer interested in her loss. Jimmy was still visiting me, with tit bits of information every now and again. With time he began to come through in a very different way; less distressed, calm, with a possible vision of his resting place. I was intrigued and carefully taking interest. He showed me a wide farmyard gate. There was still water on the right, a slight hill to the left, trees and bushes.

"Go beyond these and when you feel yourself sinking in soft earth, I'm there!" Jimmy told me. The vision was very clear. I almost felt I was in the vision. Jean phoned me. I told her what I had seen and she must have phoned the DCI. He phoned me a couple of days later - polite, pleading and almost begging me to go out with them.

"Only if you take me where I need to go", I said.

"Okay then",

On December 19th 2000, at about 8.30am the DCI and

another policeman called at my home in Cambridgeshire to collect me for my day out. It was freezing cold. The mist hung low, white frost covered the frozen earth. I sympathized; they'd already had a two hour journey.

"Please come in for tea or coffee. There is bacon and sausage on the stove. It'll only take a minute to cook some eggs", They smiled and were very appreciative of a hot snack on such a cold day.

I grabbed my coat and handbag. I had packed a disposable camera; not entirely sure why, but I thought it may be useful along with various other things that made up my cluttered handbag. With a flask of coffee we drove for about two hours. Our first port of call was Barking Police Station.

After this we went to No. 17, the house where time had stopped still for me on our last outing with the police. The vision returned.

I was asked to walk up and down the road outside. The house was of great significance, but this was all I was told.

"Ask us to stop anywhere you feel you would like us to stop", Suddenly I saw it - the farmyard gate.

"STOP!" I yelled. It was all there - water on the right, trees and bushes up a slight incline to the left. The gate was locked by a large padlock and chain. The police were out of their Range Rover in a flash and climbing over the gate.

"Stay there", they said. "No chance", I thought and I followed them over.

My pulse was racing, I was spooked. I hurried to the left, past my two companions and whizzed past the trees and bushes. I paused for breath, trembling with excitement, and suddenly I started to sink into the soft earth. I heard myself screaming. Both men raced over to me.

"It's here", I heard myself saying, and slowly they started to move the earth at my feet. Two bones were quickly unearthed. We were all in shock. I then noticed a single trainer. I asked one of the policemen to retrieve it.

I heard the DCI say we must get forensics and a photographer.

"I've got a camera in my bag. It's in the car", I told him.

"Okay. Take photos and we'll go to East Ham mortuary With this done we headed off to the mortuary. I was told to stay in the car whilst they went in. About twenty minutes later they came out carrying the bones in a wooden box.

"Well?" I said. The mortician had confirmed they were 99.9% certain they were human bones. A tibia and femur. What now? We were all subdued. The bones were human remains. How and what had become of Jimmy to be in such a morbid place? It was definitely him. He had given me such positive, clear directions.

I was elated, scared, sad, very emotional and totally in awe of all that had taken place. For the rest of my life, I will never forget that day.

The DCI dropped the other officer home then the DCI took me to his home in Chigwell. His son was home and the lad was asked to make me a coffee while his Dad checked something about the bones on his computer. I was summoned in and there was the evidence on his computer - a tibia and femur. Scary! We left shortly after. I wanted to stay at my daughter's house, but the DCI insisted on taking me back to Cambridge. I felt sorry for him because it was another four or five hours of driving for him.

On arrival at my house the phone was ringing.

"If that's Jean", said the DCI drawing me to one side, "Do NOT tell her anything. You say the whole day was a complete waste of time. Nothing happened. You must lie to her",

I could not comprehend his words. I was on a high, elated. Nothing had ever happened like this to me before and he was bursting my bubble and crashing me back down to earth.

I don't really remember the exact words I said to Jean, I was babbling nonsense whilst the detective glared at me. After I'd replaced the phone my husband immediately said,

"So it was a waste of a day?" as he had heard me saying to Jean.

"NO IT WAS NOT!" I screamed, nearing hysteria. "We found human bone, I've been to a mortuary and it's been examined by a pathologist The DCI couldn't stop me, it was all pent up. He told my husband to calm me and nothing I had said was to be repeated.

After he left I phoned Jean. This poor woman, her son was gone, and she was helplessly sitting by the phone waiting for news. I could not keep her in the dark. We chatted for what seemed like hours. I did not sleep that night.

At 8.15am the next morning the DCI phoned.

"I have just been to Guy's Hospital and seen the Chief Pathologist. He examined the bones and said they are animal - either cow or sheep. I think it's in your best interest to forget the whole day, stay quiet and don't repeat anything you saw or heard",

"Oh no", I thought. This is not the truth. I decided to do my own detective work. I found the number and phoned Guy's Hospital.

"Can I speak to the Chief Pathologist please?" I asked the girl at the end of the phone at Guy's.

"I'm sorry, the Chief Pathologist does not come on until 10am", The DCI had lied to me!

I found out he had also phoned Jean and told her they were animal bones, which seemed strange considering how strongly he had insisted I tell her nothing.

Jean and I later discovered that whilst the DCI was telling everyone that the bones found were animal, he was actually turning over the site for examination with murder investigation teams. We also learned body recovery dogs were taken to the scene on two occasions. Within two weeks of finding the bones the DCI went to visit Jimmy's mum and in the company of a police doctor had ten hair follicles removed from her head for DNA testing. For a man who did not believe the hard evidence I gave him, he showed remarkable interest in their significance.

I am thankful I have in my possession the original photos of the bones I took on my camera and a copy of the East Ham mortuary records which the pathologist stands by.

The bones were destroyed or lost and the DCI was suspended and investigated. My photocopies of the bones were examined by Home Office experts. I refused to hand over the originals fearful they would go the same way as the bones.

I did go back to the site a couple of weeks later with my daughter, but it had been cordoned off by the police.

Jean made a formal complaint about the police officer in charge of the case and has only ever given the answer of "No comment" in reference to the investigation.

8

City of London

It was a Sunday, and I was alone. The table cleared, I was going to have some fun icing the three Christmas cakes I had made; they smelt gorgeous. I always put in brandy, ground almonds, whole almonds, and lots and lots of fruit. Christmas is not Christmas without one of my cakes, according to my family.

The phone trilled out

Oh dear, I had meant to unplug it, so I would have some peace, but it kept ringing and ringing. I answered it.

"Mrs. Willcox?" a voice asked "Shirley Willcox?"

"Yes"

"Oh I'm so glad it's you - mother has just died"

"I'm so sorry" I said "how can I help you"

"Well It's like this; she has left a letter, and in it she has asked to be cremated at the city of London crematorium and she wants you to do the service. You were her favourite medium and she always went to church when you took the service"

"Please say yes - it's going to be on the 19 of December at 11.40 am. You must come to our house to discuss the hymns prayers and address. Would tomorrow at 11am be ok?"

I smiled - just supposing I had unplugged the phone!

It was an awful lot to take in. I had taken lots of services in church but never a funeral service. 19th December, four days' time- I had a million and one things to do before Christmas and all the family coming

"Are you still there?" she asked "you've gone very quiet

What does one say!!! ? I was holed in

I heard my self say "Yes of course I will do it

"Good, thank you we will expect you here tomorrow – take down our address

"Oh dear, it's half an hour away", I thought

"See you at 11am", she said, then she was gone.

"Oh My God", I thought, "what have I let my self in for?"

I returned to the cakes, but all my enthusiasm had receded, I just did rough icing like driven snow, but with Santa, holly and bells it did look good

I was ready when the taxi arrived next morning, my pad and pen ready for notes.

The family was waiting for me. No tears or sadness; they were in total acceptance of the passing.

The hymns and prayers were already chosen by (MOTHER), and the daughter and son in law asked me to mention various facts about mother's life.

Oh good, the funeral director was also present and he offered me two service books. These were an enormous help

The day arrived, and I wore my smartest suit and hat with a small veil. The taxi was early and as I set off for the crematorium the sun was bright, but it was bitterly cold with a frost in the air.

Surprisingly, considering the closeness to Christmas, a lot of people were in attendance.

The atmosphere was good

The service was going very well

The hymns beautifully sang

Silence when I said the prayers

And attentive while I gave the address

This was perfect; my first funeral service was going without a hitch.

I reached over to press the blue button to close the curtains around the coffin.

MOTHER was standing at the foot of the coffin, smiling at me.

I gasped, hesitated, composed myself, pressed the button and the coffin slid foreword the curtains closed.

I said the closing prayer, and it was done

The family rushed over to me thanking and hugging me

"Shirley we knew Mother had gone to heaven when you caught your breath; we knew then she was at peace"

I was very glad they'd asked me and very happy I had taken the service. I didn't tell them I had seen her.

10
Melvin (Yorkshire)

I had just stepped out of the shower I was dripping water everywhere even though I was enclosed in a snug towel.

My doorbell was being rung incessantly. Although I wanted to, I could hardly ignore it - it went on so long and loud.

As I started down the stairs I could see a young woman through the glass. Had it been a man I would not have opened it the door.

She was broadly smiling and went to walk in

"Hold on!" I barked. "It's 8.20 am and my first appointment is not till 9 am"

"Oh that's me", she ventured.

It was beginning to sink in, and I was not amused,

"I can hardly see you like this; would you kindly give me time to finish my toilet?"

Her face fell.

Oh dear - she shrank backwards to go back down the path.

"Am I becoming too big for my boots?" I thought?

NO, why should I feel guilty? They turn up any old time, sometimes 45 mins late, then breeze in with no apology. Am

I supposed to be at their beck and call at all times?

Then there were the constant phone calls wanting the next stage of the event of the prediction that had come true.

The phone calls range from as early as 6am, but I have even been rung at 3 o'clock in the morning, for matters so trivial is was pure selfishness.

I curled my hair with the hairdryer.

Dabbed on my make up – threw on some clothes and ran downstairs, then filled the kettle for boiling, tea or coffee ready at hand for her choice.

I opened the front door, to see that three persons were in the car outside; two men and the lady. She got out

"Is it ok now?" she smiled. "Yes, please come in" I said

"Please may I use your bathroom, we left home at 4 o'clock this morning as we live in Yorkshire –"

Oh dear "Upstairs left, first door, may I make you tea or coffee?" I asked.

"Tea would be lovely

I carried up the tray to the little room

"Are the men ok outside?" I asked

"Oh yes" she said

"Brian comes from this area -he brought us. They are going to see his sister; he was transferred to Harrogate two years ago"

"I'm so sorry I was not dressed" I said

"No it's me I'm so sorry I was early, but I was so anxious to see you I didn't think

"Why have you come so far? Are there no mediums up North?"

"Oh I had to see you - you came highly recommended and it has to be someone who could not possibly have known us",

"My husband does not believe in all this and as it's my birthday this reading is my present. He says he will keep an open mind on what you say"

I took a deep breath. I wanted this nice young person to have her evidence.

"A little boy is here. He died of peritonitis, and he is saying mummy I love you, and tell daddy I was with him when he drove the fire engine yesterday"

"Oh God, she started to cry, "if only my husband had come in - - - "

"Yesterday was the first time he has ever driven the fire engine, and when he came home his first words were,

"What would the little chap say?"

He tells me his name is Melvin

"That's right" she said

Dabbing her tears, "but his dad always called him the little chap as he was so small for his age:

"Who are …….. ?"   Melvin had reeled off three names,

"My sister's boys" she said

"He adored them; he was the youngest and tiniest and they all looked out for him"

"Melvin was our only child; we could not have any more. My three nephews are wonderful boys and they visit us all the time

"Did Melvin and his dad make 'planes out of soft wood?"

"I can't believe you're saying this. The week before Melvin passed away he and his dad finished making their biggest plane project. My husband treasures it; it is in a glass cabinet in our lounge

"Shirley, thank you so much - it is my perfect birthday present, and it was worth coming so far. I was told you would get through to him

I felt a little ashamed with myself for the greeting I had given her after her long journey and high expectation, but seeing the dear little boy with his mother gave me a lesson in humility.

11
Danny (Old Church Hospital)

One afternoon a lady sat numbly staring into space in my little room.

I had to be careful here - she looked so sad.

"We have the spirit of a dear little boy here, with the face of an angel; very fair hair and so beautiful. He says his name is Danny

The flood gates opened – she cried and cried.

"I'm so sorry", she kept repeating.

"Please don't worry

I said it was obvious she had held back her emotions for so long.

"He is my grandson. I adored and loved him so much, and he has gone and it hurts so much. I couldn't cry because I had to be brave for my daughter and son in law, as they are so broken

It was doing her good to let go. I made the wonderful stand by, a cup of tea, and she was recovering nicely

"Do you want me to go on, or shall I leave it for now?"

"Oh please, tell me everything", she said.

"Danny had a searing pain in his tummy" I told her.

"Yes"

"The appendix broke?"

"Yes

"He left hospital?" I asked

"Yes

"But the pain got worse and his mum took him back to Old Church Hospital. They saw the doctor who had operated on Danny, and the doctor said:

"The boy is spoilt - he is seeking attention. Smack him, he's not ill

The mother was not at all happy and no way would she slap her child.

Danny died that night at home.

There was an inquest on his little body

The doctor had stitched his his bowel to his scar, and the whole of his body was full of poison.

The doctor left the country - no justification for the loss of the little angel.

12
Four Ladies

It was Friday. Four ladies were due at two o'clock. I needed to pop to the shops, but if I left now I'd be back in time for the ladies.

Outside it was extremely windy and chilly. I hurried to the alley round the corner which led to a short cut to the shops. A newspaper was blowing around my feet, almost tangling me. I stood on one corner and kicked the page off me. I looked down, and a pretty face starred back at me. It was yesterday's local paper; the pretty face of a girl who had been bludgeoned to death in the road next to where I had spent my childhood. It was horrible. No one had been charged with her murder. There were no clues, no weapon. She had lain undiscovered for two weeks. I tried to put her out of my mind.

I got my groceries from the shop. I bought fish for the cat, a cauliflower for my husband as he'd told me he fancied cauliflower cheese, and fresh beetroot for me. I had done the "big shop" last evening in my husband Peter's car, but I always forget a couple of things. I hurried home. There was still time for a cup of tea before the ladies arrived.

I unwrapped the cauliflower; it was wrapped in the same news page as I had seen earlier. I took the fish from the wrapping to put in the fridge. The girl's face looked up at me again from the wrapper. The beetroot was in newspaper too, and it was leaking bright red juice. This time as her face stared at me, it was splattered with beetroot juice. It looked just like blood.

I realised this was beyond the realm of coincidence; I was being sought for communication.

Her home was close to Ilford, almost opposite the back of the C&A store. What did she want from me? Apart from four newspaper pages with her face on, I had not as yet seen her spirit or had any form of direct communication.

I chose the cleanest picture from the grocer's paper, trimmed around her face and took it up to my little room where I did all of my readings. I clipped it to a cardboard stand in full view to whoever entered the room.

My tea had gone cold, but I drank the last mouthful as the doorbell rang out.

The four ladies had arrived, three young women in their twenties, and the other lady a similar age to me. I led them upstairs to my room.

Their immediate reaction to the photo was eerie.

"She is why we've come!" one of them said. I had met them all before for readings, but did not know of their involvement with the murdered girl. She was the best friend of one of the sitters' boyfriend and sister.

There was more - another of the sitters lived in the flat next door to the murdered girl. To make matters worse, she was in at home at the time it happened and had not heard a thing.

My room had gone freezing cold. The spirit was here. She was distraught. She kept calling the name "Jon Then she showed an axe and said "He was Jamaican She showed me the flat, which was blood-soaked. It was truly awful and very scary.

The older lady knew her too. She also knew that the girl had broken up with her boyfriend who was Jamaican.

"Oh my God, he was called Jon, but no-one called him that. Everyone knew him by his nickname!"

Hysteria was rife! My room had turned into a horror extravaganza. Three of the ladies wanted to phone the police. The older lady turned to me and said,

"Shirley, you must phone the police. It's your duty

"Ladies" I said, "this is so serious we must NOT say a word to anyone. The killer, and my God what a killer, is still out there. He could come after anyone of us

We were all scared.

The girl who lived in the next door flat to the murder victim was as white as a sheet. She had gone about her life in an ordinary way, whilst her neighbour had lain dead for two weeks just the other side of the wall.

"I've seen Jon outside her home. I never liked him. Their rows were volatile and he used to hit her", she said. "I know he said he had been out of the country when it happened. But who knows?"

The spirit had definitely said "Jon", but Jon had an alibi and there was no mention of an axe in any of the newspapers.

Naturally we were all uneasy. I may be psychic, but I had

certainly not foreseen an afternoon like this. Don't ever for one single moment think that mediums' lives are a doddle.

The ladies reluctantly had to leave. It all felt so unfinished, unsettling and not what any of us had wanted. To be fair they all hugged me as they left. I had given all of them readings on previous occasions talking about happy times, engagement rings, moves to dream homes, work promotions - now this.

The spirit stayed with me. The soul who had passed on wanted justice. She was blonde, slim, and very pretty and her life had been cut short.

It must have been about five months later when she was front page news again. The newspaper told how the flat had been cleaned, about to be totally redecorated and a new central heating system to be fitted throughout. When the builders took up the floor boards in the flat a blood stained axe was found. Jon her Jamaican ex-boyfriend's finger prints were all over it.

He is serving life for murder. We were right to be scared.

13

Butcher (Barking)

Probably because I'd worked in a butcher's shop for so many years in my young life, I have always sought out real butchers to shop at. I like to see sawdust on the floor, sides of pork, breasts of lamb, trays of fresh shiny chops or liver. I don't like meat all wrapped up in cling film ready priced. There was a wonderful farm butchers in Barking.

I didn't mind the journey as I always was a good walker. Down the alley with my trolley to catch the 169 bus that took me right there. I'd buy legs of pork and lamb, breasts of lamb - my favourite, and it was the only place you could get a whole uncooked ham with the bone in, not like today.

Very content with my goodies I'd walk along to Barking station. I'd take a bus or taxi, whichever was available first.

That day I'd forgotten was a 'go-slow' strike on the trains so buses and taxis were scarce, but I wasn't worried. The day was my own, and I had plenty of time to spare. There were no taxis at all, so I took a seat in the bus station and patiently waited.

Directly opposite the station was a café. I could see the spirit of a man was drifting in and out of the upstairs windows. I was intrigued. He was dark haired, large framed and about forty-ish. He didn't go left or right, but he just kept wafting in and out. I glanced at my companions in the queue next to me, but they were oblivious to what I was witnessing. Either my thirst for tea or my curiosity got the better of me. I can drink tea and coffee for England, so I crossed the road.

The door was jammed or very stiff. I pushed hard, but it did not budge. I could see a man inside; he was tidying the tables and the light was on. I rattled the handle, and he noticed me and moved towards the door. The spirit who I'd seen upstairs was behind him. On closer inspection the spirit was bruised, a bloody hole in his chest. Before I knew it I blurted it out:

"A man has been murdered upstairs on these premises. He was shot. It must have happened 15 or 20 years ago. But I've seen him upstairs and he's behind you now

"Oh God, he's always here", said the man who had been tidying the tables. I'd changed my mind - I did not want tea or coffee; just a hasty retreat, I was feeling so spooked. Seeing my bus arrive across the road I made my excuses and dashed out. "How do you know about him? You say you've seen him? Can you make him leave?" the man asked me as I dashed towards the door.

After heaving and dragging my loaded trolley across the road I was on to the bus and grateful to be heading home. I never know what the day will bring. *Could* I have made him leave??

14
Butcher (Work)

It was October. I still worked at the butchers shop. I was about 19 years old. The day started with a dull ache in my right side. My walk to work was about a mile. By the time I got there I felt a little sick.

I sat at the till, took money, smiled a bit, and growled a lot and suddenly it was lunchtime. "Oh good", I thought, but it was a long walk back home.

I got home but I didn't fancy anything to eat and dragged myself back to the shop.

No-one asked me if I was okay. I felt and looked a little green.

I finally went home at about 6pm. By now I felt awful; I was in really bad pain and a little dizzy. The doctor was just across the road and my mother took charge and took me to him.

He was brief, to the point, no nonsense.

"Go home" the doctor instructed, "collect your night things. Your appendix has burst", I was very poorly and an ambulance was phoned for.

I spent 5 hours in the operating theatre. I know this because every time my family phoned, they said I was still there. Meanwhile, I was experiencing some very exciting phenomena.

I was travelling at a very rapid speed through a long, long tunnel. Finally I was on top of the world. A hole in the world so bright I was blinded by the white lights. There were lots of people holding out their arms, welcoming me to a house. The only way I can describe this house is it is like a colonial house, similar to the one in "Gone with the Wind I told them,

"This house is far too posh for me." I lived in a shabby terrace, with an awful cellar.

Suddenly I was zooming back down, and was still in the operating theatre. The doctors were working on me and I was floating around the ceiling watching. Suddenly the doctor exclaimed loudly he had found a cyst the size of a football.

I was in awe, but I'll never ever forget this although it is now over 50 years ago.

I awoke in a small room. I was very sore, drowsy and sickly. The doctor came to my doorway,

"Are you okay?" he said looking anxiously at me.

"Yes doctor, I saw you remove the football from my stomach", He dropped his notes and ran. The nurse came in.

"What on earth did you say to upset the doctor?" I told her all. She nodded and listened.

"You know all about this don't you. You've heard it all before" I said. She smiled, and I slept.

I was transferred to convalesce in another hospital. The ward was full of elderly ladies and me. In the bed opposite me was a lovely old lady named Mrs Binks. She had silver hair, beautiful skin and rosy pink cheeks. She was kind and talked endlessly to me.

Three days later I was restless and uneasy. As night came I couldn't sleep. It was gone one o'clock and the nurse passed my bed.

"Why aren't you asleep?"

"I'm not tired

"Yes you are. I'll give you a tablet to make you sleep

"No. I must watch Mrs Binks. She is going to die tonight and I want to watch", I said unaware of how tactless I sounded.

"You wicked girl", she hissed, "you *will* sleep She marched off and returned with two tablets and water. She made me put the pills in my mouth, but I didn't swallow them. Then she yanked the curtain around my bed.

About an hour later, peeping through the curtains, I watched brilliant gold lights surround Mrs Binks' bed. A golden staircase appeared above her head and she floated up the stairs. Then she stopped. She turned and smiled. I'm sure she looked over to me.

There in the bed was the other "her I know now I saw her spirit leave her body. In the morning I watched as the nurses rushed to her attendance only to find her dead.

My appendix bursting was a small pain to bear for the amount of spiritual experiences I had witnessed.

15
Jackie

No one can make a situation happen. My friend was a girl I worked with, and much younger than me. (I was a surrogate mum to the younger girl when we had a 'let your hair down' girly night out).

One day I went along with my dear friend to see a medium. I had told my friend she was going to marry the new guy she was keen on. It wasn't the most promising prediction as he was married with two kids, no job, and a bit shifty (I thought).

The medium told her something similar to what I had told her, and she was thrilled.

Now my turn –

"You must be a medium yourself", she said. "Would you mind giving me a reading?"

"Hold on", I said "I thought it was my turn

She then told me some remarkable truths; I was pleased she then said Bill was an important name to look out for.

"Bill" – yes; my father, my brother, my father-in-law, my daughter's boyfriend, and his father.

And yes I gave her a reading:

I told her straight,

"Get a divorce now, and stop being used by this awful husband

I told her much more, but her reading was private and she thanked me.

We were total strangers.

She got divorced and we became good friends.

16
Roxanne Bill and James (Cornwall)

The romance between Roxanne my daughter and Bill was going well. It was a Sunday and she had invited him for lunch. My husband, son, Roxanne and Bill had gone out for a pre lunch drink, Dominique my youngest was next door with her friend.

The day was very sunny and hot, the door to the garden where we ate was open, and the table set. I went into the garden to pick some flowers.

A very tall, very large spirit lad appeared and told me he had died in a car crash; it was Bill's friend Colin.

Lunch was good and we all relaxed but I had to ask Bill about Colin.

"Bill, did you know a very large tall boy called Colin who died in a car crash?"

"He was my friend" said Bill.

Roxanne was as white as a sheet and shaking badly. Oh dear - I was going to get it from my daughter.

This happened a very long time ago, but I'm always very careful not to mention spirits in front of Bill, but occasionally he does asks me things.

I don't drive and if I have what Roxanne calls a 'mission'

she drives me.

It was a Sunday morning and I was restless; I asked Roxanne "Could you spare an hour?" Bill had taken his mum to buy some plants. Roxanne wanted some petrol and a newspaper.

She drew up, and I was out in a flash. "I want to go to Goodmayes" I announced "OK" she said.

We passed a flower stall and I yelled "Stop!"

I jumped out and came back with an armful of flowers. "Who are they for?" she asked "I don't really know" I replied. She nodded; she was so used to me I smiled to reassure her.

I was safe with her, no questions.

We drove to the Goodmayes area and I pointed to a house. "Please stop here" I asked. I then gathered the flowers and walked up a very long path.

A lady opened the door to my knock, a total stranger.

"Are you Mrs. Colegate?" She nodded.

"These flowers are from Colin" I said. She replied: "it's my birthday today

I had tracked down Bill's friend's parents.

Roxanne and Bill were married; a pretty wedding with Dominique as their bridesmaid.

We did not have to wait long to break the news I was going to be a nanny, I was over the moon, delighted. I was even early for work next day!

I worked in Bodgers, a store opposite Ilford station, on the hosiery department. I told all who would listen my wonderful news.

We were mostly part-timers, and with my calculation of baby's arrival I booked my holiday.

It wasn't my favourite job, and I spent most tea breaks and dinner breaks giving readings.

Our first beautiful grandchild James was born by section at Ilford maternity. They were still in hospital when Diana and Charles got married so we had a double event.

However, my bubble burst - I was not needed to do any chores at the new parent's home. They wanted to be alone with baby.

As we were surplus to requirement we booked a caravan in Cornwall. We were very lucky to get it as it was high season.

Yes, I was a little peeved - after all I did know everything about babies and had such high expectations.

We headed West - the weather was glorious, the sky blue, sun hot and the scenery unbelievable.

The caravan was on a low cliff overlooking the sea. It was spotlessly clean, and next door was a lovely young family; a tiny new baby boy, a little girl of two and mum and dad.

I think other family members were on site, as often I saw an older woman pick baby up to take him from his pram.

"That will be my role soon I thought.

Peter, Dominique and I were enjoying a restful peaceful holiday.

I peered, watched and gazed lovingly at the little family next door.

At 5am on the Thursday morning, I woke my husband.

"I must go next door - the mother of the baby is dead!" I was pulling on my clothes.

"STOP!" he yelled "are you mad? You can't start this silly psychic stuff here.

I was out of the caravan in a flash,

A car drew up and a man got out. "I'm a doctor. Will you come to Reception with me to get the keys to this caravan; the girl there has died

My bleary eyed husband, looking very sleepy in his pjymas at the door of our caravan, watched me drive off with a complete stranger at 5am.

We were asked to look after the husband and his father while other family members looked after the children.

Dad and son were quietly sipping tea sitting on our sofa, when the dad started to cry uncontrollably. I got a wet flannel to mop his brow. While I was doing this the wife appeared and said "thank you", then was gone.

I was numb; this had all happened to me before. It is the strongest feeling of deja vu I had ever experienced.

A Hearse arrived to take away the body; such poor taste at a holiday camp. Why not use an ambulance?

Two years later I was at home with James as Roxanne had returned to work. I was a full time medium now, but minded baby too.

He was fast asleep so I sat with my cup of tea to watch an episode of Poldark (filmed in Cornwall).

Suddenly by my TV was the beautiful spirit of a girl; the mother who had passed away at the caravan site. She smiled and was gone.

I was dithery, and raced upstairs to get my diary.

 Yes - I knew where to look; James had just arrived in our lives.

The date in the diary was exactly two years ago.

She had evolved and found peace in the spirit world.

17
Richard

My second born was Richard. He was a wonderful child; blonde, blue eyed and very good.

When he was two weeks old I started to cry non-stop and I told my husband:

"He has kidney trouble",

The boy had lovely beautiful skin and he was as good as gold. I cried for four days, convinced he was ill.

My poor husband must have thought I was mad because baby didn't look ill; he looked fine, so I dried up and got on with life.

By the time Richard was seven years old he had had flu symptoms three times and had been on medication, then shortly after got ill again. This time it went on for six months.

He was delirious with fever, sore throat and a very hot head.

I had had enough

I wasn't an over protective mother wasting the doctor's time, but I was ready for battle.

I 'phoned my doctor; he was away but I was told I could bring in my son to see the locum.

He was straight to the point - Richard must see a specialist at Westminster Children's Hospital.

With the letter duly posted, I awaited our appointment.

I only waited one week, Richard was admitted for tests.

I was sorry for Richard and myself. The world was a very sad place full of dread.

Like all mums waiting for results on children in hospital, I was anxious and scared.

I could collect Richard and see the specialist the following Monday.

The specialist said Richard had been born with a defective right kidney, but with care of diet and medication he would be fine, although an operation could be required later in life (I had known this at two weeks old).

This wasn't as serious as we had thought - I was elated.

In the ward were four little boys in a row: Robert had had open heart surgery, Tony had cystic fibrosis, Danny had terminal cancer and Richard had kidney problems.

I had walked in feeling sorry for myself, but I walked out thanking God for such wonderful news, and I felt very grateful with life that day. Richard is fine now, married and the father of four wonderful boys.

18
Granny Died

We all loved our grandmother - she had shiny black hair in a long plait wound around her head, high cheek bones and, I always thought, a very pretty face.

She was wonderful; she always brought us treats, and she was the one person from my childhood I truly loved.

Granny wasn't well, and she was coming to live at our house. She was going to sleep in the room downstairs. She was always in her room and we hardly ever saw her and we were always told to be quiet.

I expect it made a lot more work for our mother, but when we are young we don't understand about these things.

We girls did lots of chores; as young as six I ironed all the shirts and peeled an enormous pot of the daily potatoes for the whole family.

One of my sisters always polished the bathroom spick and span but our mother was always cross.

One day we were running down the passage, giggling.

Suddenly I saw granny float through her bedroom door.

"Granny's dead!" I shouted.

We all stopped; silence fell.

My mother pushed through the group of us, grabbed me at my shoulders and shook me very hard.

"Stop saying such wicked things" she screamed at me.

I felt the sting of her large hand on my face.

She opened the door to granny's room.

My grandmother was almost falling out of the bed. She was very still; she had gone.

I was an odd little girl; I used to see lots of people coming out of the walls. Some of them I thought of as my friends, and I was never afraid. One of my favourites was a lady who used to dance with a long scarf, and there was a nun who was always with me if I was afraid.

I kept this all to myself - it was my very own secret; I had been hit many times for telling what I had seen.

19
Swannington (Linda Barrett)

Peter and I always took the kids and grandchildren on holiday. We were a little posher now and had upgraded from caravans, and I loved to book a cottage.

I could choose a place with my dream of an Aga. I loved cooking, and catering for my family was wonderful.

We all like a log fire, and we usually spent the evenings talking, playing board games or charades.

One particular cottage was attached to Swannington Manor in Norfolk, where we had the use of the swimming pool set in magnificent grounds.

The cottage was opposite a pretty church with a small cemetery. Nights in the country are black, so we all had emergency torches. The house was enormous; our bedroom had sloping floors and for comfort and conveniences I put my bed by the window, with Peter at the far side of the room on flat flooring.

I woke in the silence of a very strange atmosphere. The window was open wide, and the moon was very bright in the back sky with the stars shinning like diamonds.

A flutter of white across the road.

Now I was fully awake, and looked out of my window.

A young slim dainty girl in what looked like a night dress. With long hair flowing around her shoulders, she only looked 10 or 12 years.

What was she doing out alone, I must help her. I was ready to wake the house and go out.

But she vanished.

I was suddenly scared- I shut the windows, pulled close the curtains and went under the blanket with my torch

What a fool- but I suppose sometimes even mediums aren't always rational.

Next morning I was up early, with breakfast cooked and warming in the Aga. I asked Vikki aged 3 and James if they would like to pop out for a little look at the church till everyone was ready for breakfast.

"Oh what is nanny up to" said my suspecting daughter Roxanne. "I'll come too

We crossed the road and went into the church grounds.

I kept looking back to my window; it was in my direct line of vision. Then – there on the gravestone - LINDA BARRETT aged 10 years old.

Spirits usually return to earth on the anniversary of their passing hold on, the date was yesterday, a coincidence.

When my first daughter was born, my mother in law, father in law, and sister in law, all suggested I called her, Linda but, I named her Roxanne Louise. This is strange, as her married surname is BARRETT.

I showed her the grave - she knew we had almost called her Linda.

"You are strange, mum" she said.

Coincidences are very real.

20
Two brothers

Over the years I have seen several famous people, but underneath all the glamour, they're human and seeking just like us.

Yes I have met some wonderful people whom I have seen over several years, I am human too and I have my favourites.

Quite some time ago a pretty fair haired, very composed lady with a lovely young daughter, came to see me in Gant's hill.

A young lad had died in a car crash, and he mentioned a ladies name; this lady had stopped and held his hand at the road side as he passed to spirit.

He was the son and brother of my visitors.

The mother was dignified and compassionate - how do you tell a mother about her seventeen year old son who was out for a spin with his friends; he wasn't the driver but the one who was chosen to go.

His mother never asked why.

The lad had given us lots of laughs, with his caterpillar boots, tormenting the cats.

(Cats are very psychic and know if a presence is there).

There were lots of messages for his sister, turning pages at the piano when she played, predictions about her career in modelling, acting, television and films.

Our lives all stood still when the other son passed.

The family lost their second child to spirit at 23 years old.

I had a call from the mother. It was very early in the morning in the winter time, and she was understandably nearing hysteria. I too was out of my depth.

This was so wrong WHY ! WHY! WHY! - a brilliant young man in the stock exchange, a bright future, the world at his feet.

I was so angry he had been taken, but my heart went out to the family, I hadn't met their dad, but knew from the two girls that his grief was enormous.

No one can ever account for when our time comes, but I always feel it is mapped out at birth.

Mother and daughter visited me often, and on one occasion the boys told us the sister would be in Emmerdale (Yorkshire TV). The television company auditioned 1,500 young hopefuls, all vying to appear in the TV soap.

The boy's young sister was in the last 10 contestants - a remarkable achievement, and she was filmed on the Emmerdale set.

Another prediction-

She would go to the Fame School in New York.

This seemed a little far out and I cautiously gave the news in my reading to her-

I know I open my mouth, and then my brain questions

it. She did win the place at this very famous performing arts college, so envied by all hopeful young up and coming stars.

Lucky girl - what an achievement. The college is quite near to Ground Zero; I remember her 'phoning me and telling me about the intense sadness in the atmosphere around it.

She has moved on and is now doing well on adverts, film and TV. I am sure her brothers are very proud.

The boys always visit at readings for their mum, giving messages about holidays, incidents in the home and little incidental things.

I often tell the receiver of a message to please understand that there can sometimes be more importance in the small piece of evidence; it does not have to be enormous.

21
Wednesdays

My favourite days were Wednesdays.

Roxanne would drop James off at school then collect me with young Victoria.

It was always a fun day –shopping for extravagant niceties –lunch out – test drives in super cars.

Roxanne is a very competent driver and loves all cars- so, as Wednesday was a quiet day in the car showrooms, we always got lots of attention from enthusiastic sales persons – if they were more canny, they might have suspected two women and a child were unlikely to buy their wares. But test drives were open to all, and it was Wednesday.

I will never forget the thrill of sitting in the back with Victoria on smart leather seats.

My daughter drove while the sales man went on about the engine, what it could achieve and the various purchase deals.

I just sat back and enjoyed it.

It wasn't a complete waste of his time, as my daughter did live in hope of winning the football pools, or lotto!

It was Victoria's turn next: she was the most beautiful 3 year old you have ever seen, and her dream was to be a bridesmaid.

Yes, there was an aunty she hoped would get married, but no young man had been reigned in yet.

So granny took Vikki into all the large bridal departments. We dressed her in the prettiest dresses and hair accessories and photographed her. Each year we had high hopes, but no bride needed her.

Finally, aged 10, dressed in all her glory, she was bridesmaid at her aunty's wedding wearing pretty rose pink.

She almost stole the show with her three young page-boy cousins dressed in top hat and tails aged 8, 6 and 4. (I still to this day have the store photographs).

Victoria at present is in New Zealand.

Wednesday evening was my time, with my husband off to darts, when 6 of my friends would join me for a séance in my little room. The shutters closed, heavy curtains securely drawn tight. The table bare with its bright florescent edging eerily reflecting. The door tightly closed behind, with the thick curtain drawn across it. No light at all except the glow from the table.

Seven of us sat around the table fingertips just touching. The table would sway, tip almost over, and shudder.

When we wanted an answer, a loud rap could be heard for 'yes' and two raps for 'no'.

All sitters were psychic and often one or the other of us would pick up vibes from a spirit.

One Wednesday evening an R.A.F. spirit made his presence known in no uncertain terms.

I saw Douglas Bader, and he communicated with us with

raps to our questions.

One of our sitters was an R.A.F. vet, who was firing lots of questions Another soul in an R.A.F. uniform was present; he was spelling out using the alphabet and, with our encouragement and help, we got his name.

Ronald Charles Jackson. Taken prisoner of war by the Japanese on Christmas day 1941

We were in awe - the evidence was so clear but we wanted more - could we have proof?

He told us his family was in Canada now, but we could find information in the R A F church in Holborn.

We closed our circle, as always with a prayer and a cloak of protection, and ended our evening with refreshments and discussions.

These evenings were of great satisfaction. We always had remarkable goings-on.

One evening I even levitated twice in one night; everyone witnessed it.

"Who wants to come with me to the R A F church on Saturday?" I asked. I was surprised that none of them particularly wanted to make the journey and effort to find our proof.

People often ask me how do you know this and that – believe me we must put in a little effort; it is not just given. I was hot on the trail.

I got the proof, and it was mind-blowing.

My young daughter said "I will come with you, Mum" and we made our way by tube train and a brisk walk to the church.

On entering we noticed lots and lots of enormous ledgers placed on shelves all around the thick perimeter walls. I wandered around looking very knowledgeable, and hauled out a volume.

I opened a page, and there was the name Jackson. I was trembling as I fingered through the lines.

RONALD CHARLES JACKSON, jumped out at me - this was so strange. I photographed the page, but this did not feel right - it was too spooky how I found it so easily, someone was with me.

I grabbed my child had hurried over to the rector- I was babbling and talking too fast to this poor man.

"How can I find out more information about this P.O.W.? Please help me" I asked him. "There is a family in Canada" (I could hardly mention our involvement with his spirit.

I don't like to think of the reaction I may have received)

He suggested I write to the M O D who would be able to give me all the answers.

They did.

I had all the proof I needed.

Letter dated June 1984 (see attached)

The other members of the circle were astounded; what a pity no one else wanted to seek the truth.

22

Dominique and Paul

My youngest daughter had done some modelling for television adverts, and she was registered with Sylvia Young's agency. One day I had had a 'phone call from Sylvia Young to say she wanted an update with photos and measurements.

"They must be in by Monday, in black and white, not colour", I was told.

How were we going to achieve this? There was no way I could get to a photographer in time - the model book was earlier this year and notification had been slow. However, I was determined my model should have her chance.

Richard had some friends that were going to the South Pole and needed funds. Knowing these boys were good with a camera I suggested these lads did the photos; just natural head and shoulders. They said they would love to; it was an easy way to make money.

Their dad dropped them off at our house, set up a background sheet and lots of lights, then he was gone.

The boys started the shoot but had forgotten the tripod. "'Phone home" one said, "our older brother is home on leave and he will pop it round

There was a knock at the door. " I'll go", I said.

I opened the door to a tall blonde handsome lad - he was surrounded by golden lights and huge angel wings.

A voice was saying he would die in a plane crash in three months.

I stumbled in, numb, leaving him on the doorstep.

"What wrong mum? you look ill", said Richard.

I stupidly told Dominique who was in the other room that the boy was going to die soon.

"Don't be wicked", she said. The boys saw to their brother on the doorstep, took the tripod, laughed and chatted. I composed myself, offered him tea and thanks, and he left.

The remarkably good photos were duly delivered to Sylvia Young and caught the deadline.

Dominique got several auditions and photo-shoots thanks to these very good photos.

Three months almost to the day a plane crashed in Scotland.

The older brother was dead.

He was due to be a squadron leader in the RAF. He came through at many sittings, and his parents sat in our séances on Wednesday evenings.

One Saturday Mum, Dad and his two brothers came together for a joint sitting, and the pilot came through immediately.

"He is happy about the ring" he says "it's a beauty", I told them. "What's all this then?", their dad said.

"Oh dear" said the first brother "my girlfriend does not know yet but I'm going to ask her to marry me",

I gave them a cookery book, and wrote inside, 'With love from big mouth'.

We had many happy séances; their pilot came through with many accurate messages.

His best friend, the other pilot he flew with the day he died, lived in Scotland (two planes always flew together) and we were told that was wife is pregnant and due to have the baby in the August of that year. I picked this up in the early February and told the pilot's mum, and she immediately sent a pretty pink dress to Scotland for the couple.

We heard the news of a safe arrival of a baby girl mid August.

23
Adam Faith

When we first married Peter and I rented a flat in Harrow on the Hill. It was one of two rows of flats above a shop next to an Odeon cinema.

Lots of bands, singers, and performers regularly appeared at the cinema, and the audiences were often rowdy, hysterical and over-zealous.

This particular week it was the turn of Adam Faith. I had hoped I may get a glimpse of him either at the back or front of our home. At the back the extensive car park was crowded with youngsters leaving their vehicles to go into the venue.

I just knew we would see him.

I watched carefully front and back, but no luck. We watched television for the evening and it was time for a night cap. Suddenly there was an enormous commotion outside:

Shrieks, screaming, running footsteps; then a thunderous crashing at our door.

I was so stunned I opened it; and a frightened wide-eyed white-faced male rushed in and closed the door tight.

"Don't make a sound" he said he was quivering with fright.

"What the hell is going on out there" my husband had

rushed out in to the hall.

"Oh it's you!" he exclaimed.

Adam Faith had crossed our threshold.

"I m so sorry to barge in", he said "They are baying like wild animals on the attack. Please let me stay here till it quiets down

"Yes of course" we were delighted he had chosen our door.

"I'm making cocoa - would you like some" I asked "Yes please, I'd love some - my old gran used to make it for me We all sat quietly in the lounge as he tucked into a fat sausage roll with his drink and chatted about all sorts; he was so friendly to talk to. "You must accept some tickets for my next show - I'll see they're posted to you He jotted down our name and address.

The crowds had dispersed, and the chauffeur and large limo were waiting patiently for the performer. Adam Faith graciously thanked us, but it was us who felt honoured with his visit.

The tickets did arrive; we were thrilled.

24
Marie Payne

A long time ago a friend phoned me.
"You've heard about missing Marie Payne haven't you Shirley?"
"Yes of course", I answered.

A little girl had gone missing. She had been missing for at least a month and there was no sign of her. She was about four years old and had gone missing on her mother's birthday. The child had been left with her sister and she had allowed her to go across a field to play on the swings after which she hadn't been seen again.

The friend of mine said, "The mum is now seeking help from mediums. Would you like to help?"

"Yes certainly This is one thing I would never refuse help with. It's every parent's worst nightmare and if you can assist you do.

"I've given her your telephone number", my friend said.

About two days later the lady phoned. She thought it would be easier if I went to her house.

My husband drove me to her house. He didn't come in, and as he's not involved with what I do he sat in the car and read his newspaper.

Inside the house the atmosphere was very edgy. The mother looked dreadful; the dad was there, the Nan was there. They were all totally distraught.

I was trying to pick up on the atmosphere and wait to see if anything came through. The mother handed me the child's coat. As I held the coat I saw the spirit of the child standing by the television and I knew she had gone to spirit.

She showed me a rash inside her leg and she was scratching it.

"Did your little girl have some eczema?" I asked.

"Yes she was smothered in it", the mother said. "We had to keep her nails cut short because she was always clawing at her legs

"What about a pretty blue checked dress?" I asked.

"Yes, that's her favourite", said her mum.

The girl was showing me three dresses, then I described another white dress and she kept hiding behind it where there was a tear.

"I'm seeing a white dress covered in small pink roses and there's a tear on it

"That's her favourite too", her mother said.

You can't suddenly make these things up. The child was there; she was showing me things, this was real. None of the others were noticing the child standing in the corner. Suddenly she was gone.

I held her coat. I was trying to stay very calm and reassure the parents that the police and everyone else were doing their best for their daughter. I couldn't possibly tell them I'd seen her spirit. The body hadn't been found. They were hoping someone had taken her and hadn't returned her yet.

The spirit had reappeared. She was now standing in the window. The name 'Colin' kept coming through to me.

"Do you know a man called 'Colin?'", I asked.

"Colin's her brother", they said. I didn't feel this person was a child - I felt it was a man.

The poor parents were clinging to every word I said. They made me feel very welcome and didn't want me to leave, but I could see my husband walking up the garden path. I had been there nearly two hours and he had a darts match that night and wanted to go.

I promised the family I would return and try and bring some other mediums.

It became a sort of ritual. Every week we would visit the family and try and tune in to find where she was and collate all our evidence and information.

The weeks dragged by and soon became months and Marie still hadn't been found.

One of the girls came up with a good idea. "Why don't we get all the mediums together and we'll have a symposium and raise some money?" The family were not well-off and obviously desperately in need of a holiday. The past few months had taken their toll and had worn them down.

I went into the Ilford Palais and had a chat with the management and managed to persuade them to get the use of the Palais for a whole day. They knew about Marie and were happy to help.

We contacted 46 mediums, and every single one was going to give their time free of charge. We were to do readings from early morning to as late as we could and all money raised was to be given to the family.

The night was a success, with lots of money being raised. One of the mediums was the Treasurer and we went round to the family and presented them with a huge cheque.

Unfortunately there was very sad news. A young couple out walking had found Marie's clothes in a hole in a tree in Epping Forest. It contained everything from her shoes to her dress and her mother had to verify these were hers.

I'll never forget the date. The child went missing on the 11th March, which was my sister's birthday. Her body was found in Epping Forest on the 8th of July, my mother-in-law's birthday.

A very strange coincidence occurred here. I was always giving readings to people and on one occasion a young woman came to my home. I asked her if she lived in a flat.

"Yes I live in a tower block", she replied.

"When you look out, you're looking down from a long way?"

"Yes", she said.

"I'm seeing a scene. There's a man polishing a car and there's two little girls

"They're my daughters

"One looks about two; the other about four

"Yes. They always go down and play whilst Daddy cleans the car on a Sunday

"I'm not happy", I told her. "I can see a man with straw coloured hair. It looks odd, almost like a scarecrow. Please be very careful. I don't want to alarm you, but it looks like he's holding the children's hand and leading them away. He looks like he could almost be a clown or a scare crow

"Oh god, I don't like the sound of that" she said. Then that was the end of the conversation and nothing more was said.

This lady came back to see me a while later and told me what had happened.

One Sunday as usual her husband went out and washed the car, taking the girls with him. She was upstairs ironing and for some reason she went over to the window, peeped out and saw a man with straw coloured hair leading her daughters away to his car.

She began bashing on the window. She then grabbed hold of the iron and bashed it on the glass smashing the window. She yelled down to her husband,

"LOOK! LOOK THE CHILDREN! GRAB THE CHILDREN!"

Her husband, unaware of the man leading the girls away, quickly rushed over and grabbed the girls back. He saw the number plate of the car as it sped away and wrote it in the snow that had fallen on the windscreen of his car. They immediately phoned the police.

This was the man that had murdered Marie.

The police went to his home and in it they found lots of photographs of Marie the day she died and lots of pornographic photographs of other children.

This was an extremely strange coincidence.

I went to the funeral of Marie at the family's request. They asked me, along with another medium, to attend.

There were all sorts of people present - family, friends, television reporters. As we all walked into the front room and saw the small white coffin I will never, ever, forget, the whole room had a beat like a heart, it was like everybody's pulse and heart was beating as one. It was the strangest most extraordinary experience. I have never experienced anything like it before or since.

Marie has gone and she rests in peace. I stayed friends with the family for many years after.

I send all my love to this family

25
Doris Collins

A new Spiritualist church had been built in Grove Crescent, South Woodford. There was a lot of buzz about it. It was a stunning building and in our neck of the woods the spiritualist churches were tiny; some of them were former labour clubs or old halls, but this new church was a bright star.

A friend of mine asked me if I would like to go along to the inauguration service. A very famous medium was going to be there and she was going to give the service. We had never seen her before, but had read about her in newspapers and she was well known for entertaining very famous people like Michael Bentine. She had written books and had appeared in several churches so we decided to go along to see her.

We made arrangements. It was to start at 7.30pm the following Thursday evening. My daughter Dominique was going to come along too. On Wednesday my friend phoned:

"I'm so sorry, I won't be able to go. Something's come up. I'll have to cancel

"Not to worry", I said, "I'll see if my husband can drive me over instead

My husband and I led totally separate lives. His hobbies were darts, snooker, and going along to the pub to chat to his mates. Because of his hobbies, it always gave me total freedom to do as I liked and get into the spiritualist movement.

Lots of friends often said to me: "What about your poor husband? How can he put up with all you do?"

But he always had his hobbies a long while before I started going into spiritualist churches.

I asked him to take us.

"I've got a darts match that night. Where is it?"

I told him.

"Well it's a bit out of the way. Make sure you're ready on time and I'll take you over there

We set off with our instructions on how to get there, but we hit a lot of traffic and seemed to be crawling along at ten miles an hour. I desperately wanted to be at there by 7.30pm. I kept looking at the clock on the dashboard thinking, "Will we make it? Will we make it?" The traffic lights were against us at every stop. Eventually we drew up at the church two minutes before it was due to begin.

Dominique and I dashed out of the car.

I ran to the big, new shiny door; it was closed. This can't be right", I thought. I turned the handle; it seemed locked. I couldn't believe I had come all this way and could not get in! There were lights in the church and the organ had just started to strike up. I knew the service was going on. I knocked on the door; no answer. I bashed on the door. Eventually the lock clicked and someone opened it.

"How dare you knock and rattle at this door! We have a very famous medium in here and she's opening the service of inauguration", a man yelled at me.

"Yes I know, I've come to see her", I explained. "How dare you lock a church door! I thought churches were supposed to be open and welcome to those who want to come in?" I said back, annoyed at the way he had spoken to me. He reluctantly let us in.

I glared at him and we hurried to a seat. The church was very big and lovely.

The service was okay. I watched and I listened. I wasn't in awe of the medium. I don't wish to sound unkind, but it felt like quite a lot of fuss for one person, if I'm honest. It just didn't feel very 'special'.

Having been shouted at from the very beginning probably didn't put me in the best of moods either, to be honest. How did they expect the dwindling numbers in church attendances if that was how they behaved towards the congregation? I thought a church was to welcome people.

Feeling deflated, we took a taxi home.

When we arrived back my daughter said to me,

"That wasn't very good was it mum?"

I couldn't help but agree with her.

I returned to the South Woodford Church a few months later. This time, I was the medium who was taking the service.

The same person who had locked the door at the inauguration service greeted me and showed me into the mediums' room. He wanted to know if there was anything he could get me for the service, or would I like tea or water while I was waiting to go into the Church.

"No", I thanked him; he obviously had not recognised me as the person he shouted at, and asked me how dare I knock on the locked door.

Before I started the service I told the congregation how sad I was to have been locked out of this church, even though I happened to be a medium. I hoped it would not happen in future.

After the service, several people thanked me for bring this point to notice. It was a bone of contention with some of the church elders.

26
T. B. (Clive)

I t was a Monday and I was at home. I knew I had a young lady and a gentlemen coming to see me at 1.30pm, but I had the rest of the morning to myself.

There was a tall slim man in spirit hanging around my house. He was young, with dark curly hair. He had a nice smile, but a chipped front tooth and was following me around my kitchen.

"My sister's coming to see you today", he said. "She's got lovely long brown hair, and she's slim and pretty, but she smokes too much", he told me.

I smiled. He disappeared, then came back again at 1pm so I was quite anxious to see what his sister looked like. He had already told me he had passed on a motorbike. I waited for his sister's arrival then dead-on 1.30pm she walked up my path with a man.

This girl had short hair though. As she knocked I flung open the door.

"Why have you had your hair cut?" I blurted at her.

"What?" she said.

"And your brother's here", I continued. "Did he die on a motorbike? Is his name Clive?"

She was quite flabbergasted. This was all before she had even walked over my step. I usually let people come in and make themselves comfortable before we start!

"Crikey. I need a fag", she said. "I can't believe what you've told me

We laughed and sat down. She told me she had a brother called Clive, that he had passed on a motorbike and she had only just had her hair cut short.

He appeared again and I repeated what he was telling me.

"He drove up a hill, glanced round to look at his friends and at the top of the hill was a lorry - he went into it and passed into spirit

"Yes, that's right", said the girl.

The young man who had arrived with the girl was also very pleasant. His dad suddenly popped in, and showed me he had died of a heart attack.

This pair were nice. They had only been friends a short while, but suddenly I was telling them that they'd marry. They both laughed.

"We've only known each other two minutes! We're just friends, nothing more But I knew otherwise; her brother and his dad were telling me they'd marry and eventually have two children. (The words came true. They got married and had two lovely children).

The girl and her friend left.

She returned on another occasion with her Mum.

Clive came through again; he was rather anxious. Mum and daughter both worked as machinists. He kept talking about Tuberculosis and a terrible cough.

A short while after their visit, unfortunately both mother and daughter caught TB. Luckily it was caught in time and they both made a full recovery.

Spirits are so clever. We should listen to them more often as they are usually so accurate. I don't know how they do it, but it never fails to amaze me.

27

Jamaican Girl

I used to know a very lovely Jamaican girl. She was pert, vibrant, and lit up the room. She would come to my house, go up the stairs and flop into the chair.

"I love coming here, Shirley", she said "I can be myself. Nobody is watching me. I can say and do as I like I knew exactly what she was talking about. Her boyfriend was a very jealous man. If she so much as glanced at a man when he was driving the car, it meant a slap when she got home. If she chatted to anyone, it meant a good hiding and she had had many of those. I felt scared for her.

"You've got to 'tone' it down", I advised her.

I was referring to her dress sense. Her skirt was the width of a hair band. She wore minute little tops showing off her midriff. She was toned and had wonderful legs, there was no question she had an amazing physique. She wore big platform shoes and would wiggle when she walked like a catwalk model.

"But why Shirley?" I'm young - I'll do what I want", she protested.

Her youngest child was about 18 months old and her other child had just started school. Getting ready in the mornings to do the school run, her boyfriend would leave out clothes for her to wear- trousers, long baggy t -shirt tops that covered her to the thigh area. No cleavage or legs were to be shown. But she was determined to stick to her style and would go out and buy her own clothes anyway, returning from the school run and changing into her own things and go off visiting friends and family.

"I can't change who I am. This is me. This is who he fell in love with", she said. Whilst I agreed with her in principal, I had a nagging doubt inside me and still felt very scared about it all.

"I'm being serious. I think he'd kill you. Has he ever held a knife to your throat?" I asked.

"Yes, he's done it several times", and she laughed an unforgettable trill laugh.

"Aren't you scared?" I said.

"Yes, but it doesn't do to show him", she replied. "We always kiss and make-up but he does get very spiteful. He broke my nose once

I failed to see why such an attractive, intelligent girl would tolerate such a man and it upset me to imagine him mistreating her so badly.

I never saw her again. One day she went to collect her child from school not wearing her jeans or long tops. It was a hot summer's day and she was wearing a short skirt and high sandals. Her boyfriend came along and stabbed her to death outside the school gates in front of her child in the pushchair and all the other mothers and children.

I want to cry when I think of this young lady because

she was so lovely. Her boyfriend had been in trouble before for other extremely violent attacks but, even so, he only got a two year sentence. He is out and about and she is sadly gone forever.

28
Department of Environment

One morning I noticed a very large car across the road. There was a man sitting inside it. He glanced across at my house a couple of times then he drove off. About ten minutes later he came back. Then after a short while he drove off again. Then all of a sudden he returned but parked the car in a different position.

I was looking out the window for a couple of ladies who were visiting me who had not been before, and did not have my house number. As it was, they walked up my path, having found my house by its distinctive garden.

We went upstairs and started the reading when suddenly there was a heavy rapping on the front door. I was half expecting it to be the man sitting in the car and had I been in the house on my own, I probably wouldn't have answered it. But feeling a bit brave as the two ladies were here I went downstairs and opened the door.

"May I help you?" I said to the smartly dressed man standing on my doorstep.

"Yes, what's going on in this house?" he demanded.

"I beg your pardon?"

"Two ladies came in this house. Who are they?" he said

accusingly. He was starting to annoy me.

"Why? What's it to you?" I said back to him.

"I want to know who they are", he said.

"Perhaps they are my daughters. Maybe they're my sisters. What has it got to do with you?" I didn't appreciate the way he was speaking to me on my own doorstep.

"I'm from the Environment Department, Ilford council", he said smugly. He went to barge in my front door.

"Excuse me - where do you think you're going?" I stood in his way. "I'm a member of a very large family. I have lots of people visit me and that's my business

"We've had a report about you. People come and go in your house quite a lot", he said.

"Yes they do. Especially of a night when my husband is out", I said with a wry smile.

"Don't try and be funny", he answered back.

Actually, it was true; people did come and go from my house, often when my husband was out. I couldn't help but tease this man who had clearly no idea of what I really did.

"I want to see these women who came in earlier" he demanded.

"Alright then", I agreed. I had nothing to hide and showed him into my house. I wasn't afraid of him, although he looked a little wary of me.

We went upstairs to my little room. It was a tiny room, just a box room, and all the walls were covered in photographs that people had given me of relatives and loved ones in spirit who had come through to me over the years. There were also some 'thank you' letters and cards from people who had visited me, along with a few newspaper cuttings that I had appeared in over the years. There were two crystal balls on the small, round table, and various other knick-knacks scattered around the room. He marched into the room.

"What's going on here? Has any money exchanged hands?" he asked the two ladies.

"No, no", they both replied.

"What has she been telling you?" his questioning persisted..

"Well, actually, she's marvellous", one of the ladies said to him. "She's told us all about our cousin who was murdered. She told us how it was done, his name, the date, all the names of his daughters. Erm…oh yes, and she's told us about our aunt who died of a heart attack", she finished with a smile. "And then you interrupted us

He looked a little taken aback. He turned to me.

"What else do you do?"

"How long have you got?" I said.

"You are being very sarcastic", he said.

"No I'm not. If you would like to take a seat I will show you exactly what I do I asked the ladies if they would be kind enough to draw the heavy velvet curtains behind them at the window. I closed the door behind me. I turned the light off and removed the cloth that was covering the table to reveal the luminous glow-in-the-dark paint which was painted around the rim of the table. It gave an eerie glow in the pitch darkness of the room.

"If you watch the table carefully it will probably begin to rise on its own. Ooh and also if things start flying about don't worry. Now if you hear any voices I will do my best to understand what they are saying. Sometimes bits of paper float across the room, so watch out for those too", I said.

"I don't like this. Please turn the light back on", he gabbled.

"No. You asked what I did and I'm showing you. Sit quietly and watch", I said calmly.

He leapt up and nearly knocked the table over. I turned on the light switch.

"I don't like this. Are you a witch?" he asked me.

"No. I'm a clairvoyant medium. I take services in spiritualist churches too if you want to check up on me

"I'd like to go now. I'd like to go", he stammered.

"Well I'm not stopping you", I reminded him. "You asked to come into my home. You asked to see what I did and I showed you

"I must go. I've got to put a report in about you at the council. They'll send you a report from the town hall and I'll let you know what happens He left the room in a hurry.

I wasn't really worried if I got into trouble. I figured if it became an issue I'd do my readings at the spiritualist church instead.

About a week later I received a letter from the council:

Dear Mrs Willcox

Please accept our apologies for disturbing you in your home. Please continue with whatever it is you do, and we promise you that you will not be investigated any further.

You have our full permission to continue with your activities.

> *Yours Sincerely*
> *Ilford Town Hall*

This was so funny. I laughed, or should I say cackled - after all, apparently I was a witch!

In the summer of the following year, I got a phone call. It was the man from the council who had been round the year before. Oh no, I thought. Not more trouble?

"How may I help you? What have I done this time?" I asked.

"Oh you haven't done anything. I was wondering if you would come along to my son's school fete. I've heard so much stuff about you and was wondering if you would give crystal ball readings? It would really help the school's funds"

"Are you serious?" I couldn't believe what I was hearing. The man who had been so suspicious of me, asking me a favour! "You should know, I never give readings to children under 16", I told him.

"Oh no, don't worry about it. I'm in charge of it all. If there's any problem it comes down to me", he said casually.

He managed to talk me round to doing it.

It was a very large fete. On the day, I arrived to see a huge tent with a sign saying 'Come and see a spiritualist! £3 for 10 minutes'. Although this was quite a few years ago, I thought at the time this was quite a lot of money to be charging, especially at a school event. The council man collected money off people wanting to see me. The queue was enormous. He came rushing over to me.

"Have you seen the size of the queue? I've sold so many tickets. I'll tell you what we're going to do; we'll carry on charging them £3 but cut down the length of time you spend with them from 10 minutes to 5", and he turned to go off and sell even more tickets.

"But they've paid for 10 minutes? That's not fair", I said to him.

"Oh don't worry about it. More money for the school fund" he said, smiling.

I thought this was a very unfair way to treat everyone, but I got on with what I was there to do. We did raise a lot of money that day and as always in these type of events, I gave my time and services for free. However, I never offered to participate again. I simply didn't like that man from the council.

29
Paedophile

I see an awful lot of strange cases. One Sunday morning a young woman came to see me. She was very confident and full of herself. She danced up the stairs and stood in the room.

"Do you remember me?" she said.

"Erm vaguely", I replied. I saw so many people it was impossible to remember them all.

"I've got a new boyfriend, he's absolutely wonderful. I'm totally in love and so happy", she beamed.

I didn't want to shoot her down, but I was feeling very uneasy.

"Where's your daughter?" I asked her.

"She's with my boyfriend, he's looking after her. It's so convenient. He loves looking after her and always encourages me to go places and he takes care of her

"How long have you known him?" I questioned.

"Only three months", she answered. "He lives with us now

This was my cue to say something, I couldn't help myself speaking up.

"I wouldn't trust that man with your daughter. I don't

like the vibes I'm picking up", I said.

"What do you mean?" she looked confused.

"Does he ever bath her?" I asked.

"Yes, all the time", she replied.

"I'm sorry, but you've only known him three months and you're handing your little girl to a virtual stranger?!"

"He is not a stranger! We are in love, he loves my daughter and we're going to get married!" She stood up and started screaming and swearing at me. I have heard some curse words in my life, but I was surprised at the rate they spewed from her mouth. She headed down the stairs and slammed the front door behind her, but I knew I was right about what I had felt.

A long time later she turned up on my door step. It was a Sunday again. She went to walk in.

"Can you stop there please?" I said blocking the front door.

"Why?" she asked.

"I've seen the story in The News of the World. I know what has happened to your daughter. That man was a paedophile and he abused your daughter. I warned you about him and you ignored me"

"Yes, but Shirley I must see you", she sobbed.

"I warned you what was going on 18 months ago and you ignored my advice and gave your daughter to him. I don't want to see you

I shut the door and she left.

30
Gay

Once again it was a female who had come to see me. She wanted a baby. She was restless. She didn't seem happy and when somebody tries to talk about their 'perfect' marriage, I'm afraid I can be rather cynical. She had been coming to see me for a while and when she came to showing me her wedding rings, I shouldn't have, but I said,

"He's not right for you

She told me she was in love and didn't agree with me.

"I've known him for years; he's wonderful and one day I'll bring him to meet you

I could tell deep down she wasn't happy. He was working abroad in Thailand and she would go over and see him. She asked my advice; he had been offered a permanent job and wanted to sell up in Britain and for them to both start a new life abroad.

"You don't want to go do you?" I said to her.

"He's my husband and I'll do whatever it takes to keep us together. He's my life

I was thinking otherwise, but you can't very well go and say so when this young girl is sitting opposite you.

"What does your family think?" I asked.

"They think I'm a fool and keep telling me not to go

We carried on chatting and she asked me if I could see children in her future. I had to be honest with her and say I could not. It wasn't that either of them were unable to have children, I just didn't see them in their immediate future.

"Well let's hope you're wrong Shirley. But I think I've made up my mind, I think I'm going to sell up and go abroad", she said.

"I hope you're very happy and I'm wrong too", I answered.

I didn't see or hear from her for ages. She turned up one day looking strained and tired, not like the girl I remembered.

"How did things turn out?" I asked.

"Not well at all. We went to Thailand, but I couldn't get settled and wasn't happy. I couldn't get used to the climate for one thing. But my husband is earning such good money out there he suggested I get a nice place over here. I can live here and he can come backwards and forwards to me and then eventually when his job finishes we'll settle back here

No, this did not sound right to me. He seemed to be pushing her out of his life and almost paying her off. I didn't say too much, but the whole set-up sounded odd and didn't feel right. I wasn't happy with the reading and I didn't think she was either, but she thanked me and left.

Two weeks later she was back on the doorstep.

"I've been thinking. You've always told me it wouldn't work and he wasn't for me. Be honest – you're holding something back aren't you?" she looked at me intensely.

"I've known you many years and I don't think anybody should interfere with a marriage. I know you and like you and it's not my place to get involved", I said to her.

"Shirley please! Be truthful with me" she stared at me, her eyes pleading.

I took a deep breath and said,

"Okay. He's gay

"What?!" she exclaimed.

"He's gay", I repeated. "I've known it all along

"No, no that can't be right She shook her head in disbelief.

"I'm so sorry. He is gay. You will never have children with him because he doesn't want to be a father. And the idea of you settling over here is very convenient for him. He is not the sort of person that would want to "come out" and I certainly don't think he would want any of his family or colleagues to know he is gay

She cried and was understandably very upset. I made her a cup of tea.

"I like you Shirley and trust you, but I can't take any of this in. I hope you are wrong

"You did ask me for the truth and every time you've been here I've had great difficulty in not telling you that this is what's going on with your husband", I explained.

Shortly after she left.

She didn't tell me her plans, but she decided to confront him. She went home, packed a bag and caught a flight out to see him. She didn't tell him she was coming out to see him. She arrived at their home, walked into their bedroom and found him in bed with another man. That was obviously the end of their marriage.

Her husband was very generous to her financially when the marriage ended and she admitted she couldn't hate him as they had always been friends throughout their time together. He admitted he had made a terrible mistake in denying he was gay.

Fortunately, the lady went on to meet a wonderful man. She dragged him along to meet me one day and I was delighted to see that he couldn't have been more right for her. They went on to get married and eventually had two children, fulfilling the wish for a family that she had always wanted and deserved.

31
Snooker Player

The most extraordinary predictions can come true – I had seen a very young single parent for some time - she was nice; an ordinary kid of about seventeen, the pride and joy of her life her gorgeous little girl.

Life was tough for her; she lived with her mum in a council house in Hainault. No contact at all with the baby's dad. One day she arrived for an appointment with me. I could not believe what was coming out of my mouth.

"You are going to be given a brand new car, can you drive?"

"Yes, I've not long passed my test", she said. "I some times drive my mum's - car it is only tiny but a godsend, after queuing for buses and and having such long walks

I did not stop: "Your life is going to change dramatically" (this bit even I questioned). "I hope it is true but I can't change what I am being given", I said.

"You will be given your own home; a beautiful house you can choose yourself for a given sum of money

I also knew that the baby's dad was going to enter her life, and wanted contact. The poor girl was deathly white and shaking.

"It's strange, but I have never mentioned the baby's dad - I always felt you had been totally abandoned by him, and I didn't want to go down the road of nosing into private pain", I told her.

"Shirley you are exactly right. I was ordered by his mother to get lost and never to get in touch with him again. I was only 15 years old and pregnant. My boyfriend and I thought we were in love, you know what it's like at 15 and 17 years old; he did what his mother said and totally abandoned me

"Why do I pick up snooker?" I asked.

"That's him - he plays professionally. He is always on the telly.

"My god! Perhaps he has found his conscience.

"Shirley, he has never had one, or a day's contact with me or the child, but he could find me, I suppose. I'm still at the same address; no one except family, and now you, know about him

"This is going to happen soon", I said.

We were both a little apprehensive and questioning. I am not the big 'I am right', you must believe me, but this time I desperately wanted it to be true. It would be so cruel if she were to be left in limbo. Our prayers were answered in the visit of a solicitor to her mum's home.

It was all perfectly true - the house, the car, a very generous allowance for child maintenance and access to be arranged. However, before all of this could come to fruition, DNA blood tests were needed to clarify parenthood.

Bless her, this dear little soul had had only one boyfriend in her life.

I'm so happy it all worked out so well for her- it was long overdue. They did not get back together as a couple - this was never on the cards; he had moved on. My opinion of him has changed, though, and I always cheer him on when I see him on the telly, even though I don't follow snooker.

I often think of them and wish them well.

32
Exorcism (East Ham)

I n the past I have had the odd call from police to go to help sort out an exorcism. On this particular day it was our psychic circle meeting. A policeman came to my door. He'd had a phone call from a woman who was very disturbed; she'd had lots of strange goings-on in her house.

"Would you please visit her and sort this out?" the policeman asked me.

"How about it, girls?" I said to my circle of friends. Some of the girls were very keen so four of us decided to go. We jumped into one of the girls' large estate car and off we went to East Ham.

We arrived at a small terraced house in a very long road. It looked like it had stood there for years and years, but the road seemed friendly and welcoming. The policeman had 'phoned and told the woman we would be visiting, so she was waiting ready for us. Immediately, as soon as we all crossed the threshold, we began comparing notes. The place was immensely eerie. It was an old house with a long passage from the front door all the way to the back of the house. There was a cellar, two lounges and a dining room.

"Feel free to wander around", the woman said.

"I feel very drawn to the first lounge", I told her.

"Yes, that's where all the activity has been happening

It was a warm summer evening, but the room was very chilly. There was a bible on a chair next to a spindly looking table and the bible was open.

"Why is this here?" I asked.

"I put it there for safety, but if you watch the pages will start turning by themselves

Nothing happened immediately, but during the course of the evening we would notice a very fast fluttering of the pages, then it would stop and come to a rest. Then a little later the pages would flicker through again then stop. Every time it did this one of us would go over and check to see what was being shown. It was almost as if someone was trying to tell us a story. I know this sounds odd, but as a medium you do come across some weird situations.

We decided to gather close, and we recited the Lords Prayer. We also then asked for protection because it was certainly a very strange atmosphere. Immediately a spirit came to me. I asked the lady who lived there if she knew of a nurse who had a link to the house. I felt her name was Jean and she was about twenty three when she passed.

"No, that doesn't mean anything

"She's wearing the old fashioned nurse's uniform; starched blue with a white belt, and a sort of cap on her head, with a white apron and a 'Red Cross' badge pinned to her

The woman shook her head. None of this meant anything to her.

"Now I'm seeing an army man I hurried over to the

settee in front of the window. "Was this room ever used as a bedroom?" We all felt particularly uneasy standing at this particular part of the room.

"I really don't know what you are talking about. It's just my husband and I that live here

"Yes, I know, but this house has been in the family; it's part of your roots", I told her.

"Yes, that's right. Originally it was my great-grandmother's, then my grandmother's, then one of my aunts lived here and then I inherited it. There was a clause in the Will that said I'm not allowed to sell the house, and that I must pass it on and keep it in the family

The girls were whispering as they felt various things happening. One of them could smell Dettol, which linked in with the Nurse as it's the sort of thing associated with hospitals. Another one of the girls could smell boot polish and felt someone polishing heavy boots which connected with the army man I was picking up.

The bible continued to flick through the pages even though we had checked for draughts, and shut all the doors. Suddenly I felt hands around my throat and it was almost as though the life was being squeezed out of me. I was gasping and gasping. I asked the others what they were sensing.

"The air's gone very, very cold", they replied looking concerned. I asked the spirit to stop.

"We must find out what's gone on in this house", I said, regaining my breath, when out of nowhere my voice changed to very high pitched rasping tone which wasn't my own.

"You must go to your mother and find out if a nurse

called Jean lived and died in this house", I said to the lady who lived there.

"Okay I will. I don't think you're right but I'll ask her. She only lives three doors down.

"You go and ask her now and we'll wait on the doorstep", I insisted. I was determined to get to the bottom of this. The hands that I had felt around my throat had released, but I wasn't happy with this atmosphere at all.

We watched as she went a couple of doors down the road, and then emerged from the house with an elderly woman. The elderly woman was all of a fluster. She started to talk.

"Jean was my sister. She was a nurse and she was murdered in that front room. Her husband came home from the war and he suspected she was having an affair. He pushed her on to the bed which was under the window. He climbed on top of her, knelt on her chest and strangled her. Then afterwards he hanged himself, and left a note explaining what he had done and why

Although this confirmed what we had felt it still shocked us to hear it confirmed. Jean's spirit had not left that room and when we re-examined all the pages that had opened on the bible the first letter of each page that had opened spelt out the name "Jean She was desperately trying to communicate.

The ladies from the circle and I stood together closely, put our finger tips together touching and prayed for the release of her soul from that house. We asked her to go into the light, and find peace in the spirit world as she was now safe.

We left about half an hour later. Shortly after the lady who owned the house phoned me to say how different the house felt. It was no longer cold and uninviting and she was very thankful that we had come. I was pleased for her and for Jean.

33
Scotland

L ots of my wonderful psychic experiences have happened whilst on holiday.

We had gone away to Scotland. We only had one child at the time - my daughter who was thirteen months old. My husband and his best friend decided it would be nice to drive up to Scotland and amble around and see the various sights. I had always wanted to go, to see the mountains and breathe the clean, fresh highland air.

We set off on the long drive. My husband and his friend had a mate who had moved to Glasgow and settled down with his wife and baby. He invited us all to call around and use his place as a base from which to begin our travels.

Our first outing was to see the Loch Ness Monster, or at least the Loch.. We stayed at a nice little B&B then, wasting no time, headed off to the next place.

Glen Coe was a vast, desolate mountainous place. We had a picnic, and the baby toddled around, but I found the place quite eerie. We were the only ones around.

The sky was strange. One minute there were blue hues, then a dark grey mist. I then had a very peculiar experience. I could suddenly hear the sound of distant bag pipes. I turned round to my husband who was chatting to his friend, the baby asleep between them on a rug on the floor.

I wondered over to a low, stone bridge. I gazed into the distance of the hills. As the mist came down more heavily, I looked to see what appeared to be hundreds of men marching along in kilts down a valley. On the other side of the mountain I could see even more of the men. I couldn't take it all in. I felt like I was living a nightmare, there were screams and yelps and it was creepy.

I closed my eyes then turned to look at my husband who was still chatting normally to his friend. I couldn't figure it out. Was I dreaming? Was I imagining it all? I was covered in a fine sweat. I looked back at the scene.

The men were waving swords and carrying shields. I knew I was witnessing a blood bath. There were not one or two spirits; there were multitudes. This was vivid, but I had seen enough.

I rushed over to my husband. "I think it's time we left. I want to go

"What? Relax, Shirl. Go and take some pictures or something. The baby's just gone to sleep, and if we go now we'll disturb her and wake her up" my husband said.

I took my camera out and photographed the baby, my husband, my husband's friend, the car, anything so long as I didn't have to look in the direction of that hill; I was too scared of what I might see again. But I could still hear the bagpipes.

"Can you hear bagpipes playing?" I asked the two of them. They looked blankly at me as

If I was mad. Psychic experiences and such things held no interest to either of them so to discuss what I had seen would have been pointless.

A car arrived and two men got out. They were further up the valley. I could see them putting up a tent right amongst where I had seen all the men in kilts fighting.

"What do they think they are doing?" I said staring at them fixing up the tent.

"They're putting up a tent. It is allowed, you know", my husband answered.

"What an awful place The words came without thought.

"Are you serious? This place is stunning. Look at the scenery - it's everything you've been asking for My husband couldn't understand my negative attitude to it all.

As I watched the two young men struggle in the wind with their tent my motherly instinct kicked in. I wanted to run over and tell them to pack up and go home, this wasn't a safe place to be, but knowing they would think I was mad and interfering if I did I decided against it. But I wasn't happy at all; I was so agitated.

The baby woke up and we all decided it was time to leave. I couldn't get away quickly enough; this place put me on edge. As we drove away I clung onto my baby and looked at the two boys hammering the tent pegs into the ground. All the spirits in the mist had now gone, but the mist had become lower and the place looked spookier than ever.

We stayed at a very welcoming B&B nearby, but I could not sleep that night. I couldn't forget the scenes I had witnessed. I was lost in thought, but my husband assumed I was sulking as I wasn't talking.

The next morning, at breakfast, we were told that an enormous storm had taken place on Glen Coe during the night. Two young men had pitched a tent and lost their lives up on the mountain. Their tent had been struck by lightening.

There must have been a reason for my uneasiness. I have never returned. Half of me wants to go back; the other half is too scared. Maybe one day I will go back and re-examine what I saw.

34
Breaking Glass

It was turning out to be a very hot summer. All morning I'd heard the song "I love the sound of breaking glass" playing over and over in my head. I don't know why I kept hearing it; I'm not very musical at the best of times, but this was coming over very clearly.

I had appointments that morning and I was waiting for people to arrive. Suddenly there was a commotion and four people were at my doorstep. There was an older woman, a couple of younger ladies and a very loud girl in a wheelchair.

"Make some space, I'm coming in!" said the girl in the wheelchair.

It was quite tricky to manoeuvre. There was the porch, a step into the living room and the doors were not very wide. I had to move all my clutter out of the way. I didn't mind accommodating this girl, but I wish I had been told in advance and I might have been better prepared.

"The reading is for me", she said firmly. "I don't want the others to hear. You can go off mother", and at her command they all marched off and drove away.

"I must ask you something", I said. "Does the song 'I

love the sound of breaking glass' mean anything to you? I've been hearing it all morning

"No. I don't even like the singer", she remarked.

"Fair enough", but then I suddenly saw and heard lots of glass shattering around her. "But I'm sure this has something to do with you

I was being shown a tall, sturdy male with black shiny hair. He was handsome, but there was a fire between him and this girl. They were yelling at each other in her bedroom. They argued and they screamed. He was shouting at her and suddenly he lunged at her, pushed her hard and she went flying through the window. She fell and landed on the concrete driveway. Her back was broken. She would be in a wheelchair for life. I relayed what I had seen.

"That's exactly what happened to me. He's locked away in prison now. But I want to know about my life and what's going to happen to me in the future", she said.

"He was your husband", I said.

"Yes. We're divorced now and financially I'm very secure, but I'm very lonely Her manner was quite abrupt and curt.

"Well take hold of my crystal ball for a while, and give me something of yours to hold and I'll see what I can do

"I'm not interested in the past and I'm not interested in spirits. I just want to know what's out there for me", she said.

After a minute or two I took the crystal ball back.

"Do you know a 'Danny'? It's coming up very strongly", I asked her.

"No. Should I?"

"Yes, I think he'll be an important part of your future. Are you Catholic?"

"No", she looked puzzled.

"Well this 'Danny' is. He's very nice, gentle soul. Hold on- you're going to have a son", I said excitedly.

"Don't be ridiculous. I'm in a wheelchair. I can't have children", she sneered at me.

I didn't appreciate the way she was talking to me. She had come to me, but was treating me like a servant. I decided to ignore her attitude and continue as best I could.

"You are going to have a boy. He will beautiful and he will change your life. The father will be Danny", I said.

"I think you're talking a lot of rubbish. I don't know what I've come here for. Is my mother back?" she asked.

I looked out of the window and saw her mother parked up outside.

"Yes she is", I said, relieved. I was glad to see her go as I felt I'd been wiped on the floor.

A couple of years later I was in Marks and Spencer. The front of the queue was a bit noisy. I noticed there was a blonde woman in a wheelchair bouncing a baby up and down on her knee. I recognised who it was and walked up to her.

"Hello", I said and the girl turned to look at me.

"Shirley!" she smiled at me. "Look what I've got!" she said nodding to her little boy. "I'm so pleased to see you. Listen, I'm so sorry for when we met before. I've always wanted to apologise to you for the way I spoke to you, but didn't think you would see me. You were right about, well about everything. I met a man called Daniel. He's Catholic, like you said and just the kindest, nicest man you could meet. And now we've got a baby together. This little boy has changed my life. He's changed my personality too. I'm no longer that angry bitch!" she laughed.

I felt so pleased for her. Things had worked out for the best.

35
Trevone

I love pretty scenery. Yorkshire, The Lake District, Cornwall and Wales are all my favourite places. I have never been abroad and we always take our holidays in a beautiful part of the country.

One day three girls came to see me. They were all related and decided to sit in on the reading together. I was talking to the first girl.

"There's a lady standing by you and she looks terribly sad. She tells me she worked as a nurse and died of breast cancer", I told her. "She's taking me to a lovely part of Cornwall. There are cliffs, a small beach and pretty countryside. It sounds like the name of the place is 'Trevone'. Does this mean anything?" I asked.

"Yes. My mother is the nurse who died of breast cancer and we have a family cottage at Trevone. It was bought by my mum and dad years ago, but we kept it in the family", said the girl.

"She's also mentioning something about a tin mine", I said.

"Yes that's correct. The family worked and owned a tin mine. It's closed now

"She's taking me back to the cottage. It's pink I looked over to the girl to see she was crying.

"Yes it is. I loved my mum so much and she was so young when she died

"I feel she is at peace and I think she keeps showing me this cottage because she loved it so much", I explained.

"She did. If my mum could have lived anywhere all the time, it would have been Cornwall. When she was dying in hospital she kept saying she wanted to go back and we promised her we wouldn't get rid of the cottage, and that we would keep it

"Is it on hire through an agency?" I asked the girl.

"Yes, we can't live there - it's a holiday cottage

"You must give me the address. I'd love to visit

"I'll give you the number of the estate agent", said the girl.

After a number of phone calls I managed to arrange a convenient date for my husband, my son and his fiancée and a friend who hadn't holidayed in years to all stay at the cottage in Trevone.

We all set off for Cornwall. This tiny seaside harbour was just past Padstow. Beautiful winding lanes, small cottages scattered around, corn fields one side, coast the other. You could stand gazing out to sea and watch the sunset. It was utterly stunning.

The first evening we were there, I had a visit from the nurse spirit. She had definitely taken up residency in the cottage. She was so happy that visitors were going backwards and forwards to her home. Cornwall is a very haunted, psychic place and she told me about a house on the harbour. I couldn't quite understand what she meant but I kept seeing a big, square house and what looked like a window without glass.

I spoke to my friend the next day and suggested we go into Padstow and have a look around. My son and his fiancée were doing their own thing so the three of us drove to Padstow. My husband was happier sitting by the harbour reading his newspaper than traipsing about so my friend and I strolled around.

I saw the house the spirit nurse had shown me the day before. It was very prominent and stood out like a sore thumb. It was a very old building and had an enormous sort of balcony area, but it created a weird optical illusion of looking like a huge window.

We headed towards the house and as we approached I saw a lady in spirit there. It wasn't the nurse; this one was much older, about 90 years. Then she was gone.

As we walked towards the gates of the house, they swung open on their own. We walked through and headed up the stairs to the balcony area. My friend took a photo of me on the balcony and I took some of her. Fortunately, she too had an interest in all things psychic.

We decided to go souvenir shopping, but went to check on my husband before disappearing off again. He was still quite happy with his paper, people-watching and sitting in the sun. I bought him a coffee and some proper seaside chips and we went off to the shops.

We went into an art shop first of all. We stood around

gazing at all the amazing paintings then made our way over to the staircase which went downstairs to more paintings.

"I wouldn't go down there love", said the man behind the counter, "it's haunted

My friend and I giggled.

"That doesn't bother us", my friend and I both laughed.

"Are you sure?" said the man. "Be careful on the steep stairs. Most people that go down there rush straight back up. For years and years people have reckoned they can feel a presence

Down we went. There were about five paintings of the big house by the harbour on the walls. They were all different sizes and by different artists. There were shadows where the window was. It was as if all the artists had either knowingly or unknowingly drawn the spirits that were there.

We moved on to a bookshop. My friend bought a book without me knowing, had it wrapped and when we returned home gave it to me.

"That's just a little thank you for taking me on holiday", she said handing me the gift.

"You didn't have to do that", I said to her.

"Open it now, go on

It was a book about all the haunted places in Cornwall and one of the first photos was of the house with the big window, and there was a description of a lady said to be haunting it. It was the same lady I had seen.

36
Photo on my wall

A photo stares at me from my wall - she is a blonde, pretty and young, I am always reminded that I should have been firmer, more positive, and made her listen to me. She does come through to me sometimes when I'm giving a reading- so the forcefulness in me comes out.

It was a Monday, "I couldn't go to work like this" she whimpered, with her black eye, a horrible scratch on her cheek by her eye, and a dreadful sore patch where he had pulled out some of her beautiful hair.

"I've taken the week off sick. I just don't care, but the girls at work haven't got any patience with me. They think I should leave him, but I love him

"He's always so sorry; he cries and apologizes and reassures me that he does love me

I'd heard it all before.

"Are you mad" I asked harshly? "You don't need a clairvoyant medium to tell you it won't work. For god's sake, have the sense to leave him

She stopped snivelling and gasped at me with large eyes. Please don't be cross with me Shirley. I like you and I feel safe here", she said.

"Look love, I care, I can't stand to see a lovely person like you, so beaten up

I wanted to cry. "I have an idea" I stated In the crystal ball I am seeing Liverpool - could you go there? Do you know anyone who lives there? Just perhaps a little break to cool things".

"Its funny you mention Liverpool; Mum moved there two weeks ago. Dad got a transfer from work and they have a bungalow on the outskirts. Dave, my fella, smashed my room and trashed the lounge in our home. Mum and dad barred him so I moved out. Mum and Dad hate him - that's why they moved; the job was on the cards, and it was a good opportunity for them - they were scared of Dave

"You little fool" I said.

No wonder I'd asked her it she were mad.

"Why do you come to a stranger for advice? When you can't take it from your parents who love you? You do know it won't stop", I said.

"Has he ever threatened you with a knife?"

She stayed silent, and I knew.

The crystal ball had misted up: this is what happens when there is no future.

This silly pretty creature would not leave him; she was so positive he would change and that he loved her. What price love.

Perhaps I gave up too easily. I didn't push anymore: I just smiled and let her go.

It happened two weeks later.

He stabbed her to death outside a newsagents in broad daylight, then calmly waited for the police.

I felt haunted for years - not in a bad way, but with the memory of such a lovely person being taken like that.

If I see anything now I'm much more assertive, even to the point of bullying. I hope she is at peace.

37

Anna

One afternoon I heard a loud knocking at my door: a black London cab was outside,and a man was yanking out cases, a bag and a pillow. He marched up my path, dumped everything by my door and said "these belong to my daughter - I hear you'll take her in

"Hold on, who are you", I asked.

"We are throwing her out - she is trouble. She's a friend of your daughter

A young girl was sobbing; she looked about sixteen.

"Please don't go, dad", she called as he was revving up his taxi and making a fast get-away.

"Don't cry love. Are you a friend of Roxanne's"?
"Yes"

Roxanne brought all the lost souls to my door, even cats, But this was a little different; I was getting a staying guest. "Roxanne will be home soon, let's take your bits in then you can tell me all about it over tea", I told her.

She told me she was Anna, but as all sorts were spilling out and she was so upset I did not note too much of the detail. We put her up on the settee for sleeping, and both my girls gave her wardrobe and drawer space. Our house was crowded but we managed, but after two months and being told by a mutual friend her parents had had a restful break in Italy for three weeks, I thought it was time to confront them.

After all, I'd given support and comfort to a complete stranger for eight weeks - what sort of parents were they?

"Anna, I need to meet your parents this evening", I told her. "Oh no, not tonight - its Friday; she has prayers and candles for Sabbath

"Does she indeed", I said.

"Oh and Shirley I'm ever so sorry to tell you but my mother hates English gentiles

Really!- My hackles were up. I wondered if this person had told her Jewish friends she had chucked her daughter out to be cared for by the enemy.

We were shown in to their home. Candles lit the lounge.

The mother was draped in a large comfy easy chair, her bouffant hair and dangling hand with long plastic false nails (no doubt the latest colour), with heavy false eyelashes flickering nervously. Her make-up was so thick I almost felt naked

"Tonight is not convenient for her to come home", she said.

I was aghast: this is the hypocrite who hated my race; this poor specimen did not deserve to be Anna's mum. The girl had been no trouble to us. I did not want payment or thanks for looking after Anna. What sort of mother was this?

I couldn't hold it in: I did try, but I was glad I told them exactly what I thought of them, and swept out, alone.

Anna stayed.

Not all Jewish women are like her or him; I have some wonderful Jewish friends. It's not our race or religion that matters. Kindness to humanity counts first and foremost.

We have all encountered insults, but hers to me I will never forget.

So many people have crossed my mat.

Famous actors, small part actors, film, TV and stage performers, boxers, footballers, cricketers, singers, models, even princess Diana's cousin, a county court judge and many police officers. They all find their way to my door by word of mouth.

There was even a young foreign prince who arrived, with six body-guards armed with guns.

I was horrified and shocked, on a bright sunny morning, to be confronted by six guns.

The prince spoke to them in a foreign tongue. He also spoke, pure cultured English to me.

I was wary, but he told the men to wait in the very large black car with dark windows and diplomatic badge. He told them he wanted to come in with me alone.

He was only 19 years old. He told me his sister had been to see me and I had mentioned a reluctant young man who was not too keen to follow in his father's footsteps.

This lad would one day be a king: he was polite, and said it was wonderful to escape and be treated as ordinary.

I offered him tea (in a mug), and he thought it so good not to be bowed and curtseyed to. I was just me. He was nice; very down to earth and human, and not at all a snob. It was a pleasure to meet him.

Another of my visitors was probably the most elegant, sophisticated Grace Kelly look- alike, and spoke with a cultured voice. Her clothes and jewellery were very expensive; the labels my grand-children would die for.

"Please don't be offended" I said but I only give the truth. "I am picking up high-class hooker

She screeched with laughter.

"How the hell did you know that,Shirl?" The common voice shocked me. "You are the only one who knows She laughed: "my friends said you were good

The accent was sort of Liverpool, and hearing the common voice, coming from her lips, was a revelation. She was a lovely ordinary girl, in the prostitute trade; she was kind and caring and very good to her loved ones. She composed her elegant self and, after telling her various other things, she gave me a hug and left.

She visited me often after that, but I worried and was scared for her.

She was almost like another daughter but I couldn't take them all in.

She was one of the lucky ones: some of the others, in the same trade, did not fare so well.

Molly - she was a total mess. She was nineteen years old, drugged up and did her trade on the streets of Leytonstone. She had had a little boy at seventeen years old, and given him up for adoption so he could have a better life. She took the drugs to block the pain of parting with her child, and sold her body to pay for the drugs.

She died age twenty one years; her friends came and told me.

Somewhere out there a little boy has a mum to whom he must be grateful.

Are our lives mapped out?

Do we have a designated path to walk?

As I've said before

Only God knows.

38

Dance School

I've always been happy to give my time freely for evenings of clairvoyance in aide of charities. My favourites were kidney charities because of Richard my son, and all the attendant hopes and dreams, and smiling faces. These charities were for terminally ill children, with brain tumors, cancer, etc. The child would choose their wish, be it swimming with dolphins, going to Disney world, on a helicopter flight, whatever, to spend an unforgettable time with their family.

The David Lloyd Centre, Chigwell, was one of the places given free of charge to help the charity, and I appeared there many times It is wonderful that companies can be so generous. I also appeared at many other various venues.

Then there was the dance school!

A young woman came to my Gants Hill home, she had moved house, was newly divorced with a small daughter, and needed direction.

"I need a job that will give me a life, and ensure that I'll be around for my child", she pleaded.

I had seen her before, and had indicated the marriage split. This young lady had been a wonderful dancer; it stood out a mile.

"Why don't you start a dance academy? You have the talent, qualifications, and who's Pat?"

"She is the girl I trained with, I haven't heard from her in two years

"Please get in touch with her", I said

"It would be a first rate success for both of you

"I hadn't thought of dancing" she said. "I've been running my own hairdressing salon

"No, not any more" I implored "Make the change

She left after I'd given the usual predictions, on love and relationships.

About eighteen months later I had an appointment with two ladies about two o clock.

I put the casserole in the oven, and covered the freshly peeled potatoes. I somehow knew the afternoon was going to be long.

It was! The ex hairdresser and her friend was both on my doorstep.

They were dressed in leotards and leg warmers.

Yes! Of course, they had come directly from the dance studio.

The dance school had taken off, big time.

This was a very enterprising young woman; she had eight classes on the go, all ages, and including elocution and drama. Well! It was almost a stage school, and in such a short time.

She emptied the contents of her large soft bag on to my table.

There were endless photos of children, all strictly uniformed in leotards and tutus, all looking very professional.

"Shirley", she gushed, "I've made it! My dance school is full with a waiting list. The drama group is budding. The whole thing has taken off. This is Pat, by the way, my friend you told me to get in touch with. She has passed all her exams as a dance teacher. She takes most of the lessons. I take some too, but oversee the whole school with the help of my boyfriend who you told me I'd meet!"

"Right!" I said, breathless for her.

"Do you remember seeing a huge pile of money?" she asked.

"Yes I do", I replied.

"Well, I've put in for a large lottery grant for the school. Do you think I'll get it?"

She certainly knew every trick, especially considering the school was apparently doing so well.

"Oh and…" she didn't stop. "We want you to do an evening of clairvoyance to give the pupils an opportunity to go to see the Royal Ballet at Covent Garden. It'll give the students a goal She finally stopped for air.

I suppose I am a sucker, especially where charity is concerned and I agreed to help them out.

By the time they had left I was drained. The dinner had cooked itself nicely so I had a little time for me, before the next two were due at 7.30 p m.

The evening of clairvoyance for the dance school was to take place in Romford. It was early December and an extremely cold Friday night. My husband took me along and said he would collect me at 10.30pm.

The hall was filling up nicely; practically every seat was gone, but I didn't know a soul. Where were the two ladies who had asked me to appear in the first place?

A young lady approached me,

"You are the clairvoyant aren't you?" she asked.

"Yes, I am. Where are the dance teachers?" I enquired.

"Oh they asked me to introduce you to the audience. Because the sale of tickets was so fast and successful the Head has taken all the staff to a health spa for the weekend on the proceeds of tonight's takings

My jaw dropped at the audacity. Here I was giving an evening of my time just so a few ladies could be pampered at a health farm!

Looking out at the sea of faces, I knew I couldn't let all these people down and went ahead with the evening. It was a great success, but I wouldn't get caught out again.

39
Bodgers

I was working at Bodgers, the department store. The girl on the wig counter stood across the store to me and there was always a young spirit boy with her, maybe ten or twelve years old, and he was always floating around her. I didn't go and ask her anything, but I was seeing more and more of this little boy. The girl looked very miserable. One day I walked across and said,

"Are you having man trouble? You do know he's got another woman don't you?" She looked at me, daggers.

"How dare you say that! My husband and I are very much in love. What's wrong with you?" She was seething with rage. Oh dear, what had I said? I hurried away.

She kept looking across at me as we were only a few yards apart and giving me horrible, black looks. What do they say - "Only fools rush in I wondered why I would always say these things. I didn't mean to.

Her husband would sometimes pop in to the shop and she would throw her arms around his neck, embracing him with her legs dangling off the floor and then reach up and kiss him on his lips. Of course I was a very strong observer. I always watched and I knew this was a very false display, but it wasn't my business.

A couple of weeks later she came over to me.

"Are you a medium?" she asked.

"Yes", I told her.

"Please could I talk to you? There are quite a few things I would like to ask I was on my guard because I had upset her before, but all of a sudden it was out of my mouth.

"Did you lose a little boy in a cot death, who would be about twelve years old now?" Her eyes filled with tears and she started to cry. "I'm ever so sorry", I said.

"No, I feel him with me sometimes", she said through tears.

"Ever since I've known you I've seen you with this child, hovering around you; not everyday, but quite often. When spirits draw near, it sometimes means there is something wrong. But can I just say I'm very sorry for what I said about your husband

"No, there is something wrong

"Listen", I said, "if you really would like me to tell you what's going on I will, but I don't think we should do it here. If you get upset on the shop floor we'll both get in trouble. Let's both arrange the same lunch hour and we'll talk in the canteen

We met up at lunch and she sat opposite me with big, large, sad eyes. Obviously I had brought back memories of her boy, but she had other worries. I thought it best we get down to the nitty-gritty.

"Your husband is seeing a nurse. She works at Guys Hospital and lives across the Thames

"You can't be right, you can't be right. He loves me", she repeated.

"Then why did you ask me? What do you want to know?"

"I know there is something wrong

"Well, this information is coming from your son. Spirits give me messages and if I am going to be blurting it out, it's got to be accurate

"Okay", she said. I suggested that if she was suspicious of him, to check up on him; be a bit of a nosey wife and see how he reacted. "I won't find anything, he'll be fine. He's a very confident man. Did you know he's a policeman?"

"Yes", I answered.

The lady went home and must have told her husband some of things we had discussed.

I was on my next shift a few days later (I worked part-time like most of the girls there), when suddenly the lady's husband came storming in. He marched up to me, and grabbed me by the collar, putting his face into mine in a threatening manner.

"You can stop right there!" I said to him, pulling myself up to my full height. "I'm not being arrested for anything and you've no place coming into my work threatening me. Would you like me to call my boss over?"

"I'm warning you, don't you say anything to my Missus

I was shocked. I don't know what she told him, but I knew you should never come between husband and wife. I didn't like his aggressive manner and the way he spoke to me.

The lady came into work later and I asked her,

"Why are you dropping me in it? Please don't use me

and ask me things if you're going to report it back to your husband. I can do without people like him coming in and threatening me. I have a husband and a son who is 6ft 4 inches tall, and he'll come and look after me!" We both laughed at this, but I wasn't very trusting of this lady.

The bosses at the shop were very aware of who I was and what I did, and every now and again I would get a warning because of whispers going around as to what I had said. I certainly didn't want another confrontation with the policeman, and I went out of my way to avoid seeing the lady from the wig counter.

One day she came over to me.

"Please be friends with me, Shirley. Things are getting very bad at home

"I'm not going to talk to you at work and I don't really want to get involved with stuff that is husband and wife business", I said.

"He's going to stay at his mother's for a few days. He won't be at home, will you please come round?" I thought about it. She had a daughter a similar age to mine and she said if we came round the girls could go off and play their records together and we could have a private chat. I agreed to go.

Between us we found a convenient time and my husband dropped my daughter and me off at her house. We sat down and I began to talk. All the truths came out and I was telling her all sorts of things.

One thing I was aware of was her home. It was as shiny as a new pin. She even had gold cutlery. There wasn't a crease in a cushion, or a mark on the carpet. The whole house was absolutely spick and span. Maybe I noticed it more as I'm naturally very untidy!

"Where on earth does your husband sit?" I enquired. "Doesn't he crease the cushions?"

"Oh I am always checking on him. He knows he has to take his shoes off before he comes in. He knows he must be tidy This I immediately thought was probably one of the reasons for their problems. You don't keep a husband in a palace! After a hard days work a person needs to relax. I wasn't at all comfortable in that home. Every time I moved she brushed the chair, she brought out biscuits on a plate then brought out the mini-vacuum cleaner. She obviously had a thing for cleanliness, but this doesn't make for comfortable living. She needed to back off and calm down.

She was firing questions at me about the nurse. I was telling her various ways how she could track him down: she could hire a private detective or she could be quite clever and follow him. She asked me if I would go with her. I told her "No I drew the line there as I didn't like the husband. He had already threatened me and he meant business.

My husband collected my daughter and me and we went home.

A few weeks later she phoned me.

"Shirley I've been arrested. I'm in a police station. I've found them. I've found their love nest…and I've trashed it

"Oh no! What's going on?"

"I don't know. I've got a solicitor and hopefully it's all going to get sorted. I'll let you know what happens

A few weeks later I heard all the details. She had tracked down the love nest. She had taken her daughter along with her; a bad move, I thought, as he was still her father after all, and the little girl thought the world of him. She had jemmied open the door and gone in. She then went to work on the house. She slashed all their clothes in the wardrobe to ribbons. She ripped open the mattress and pulled out all the stuffing. Poured shiny red gloss paint all over the bed, carpets, furniture and walls. The television was destroyed. The phone was torn off the wall. She smashed all the crockery to pieces and when she discovered they even had the same gold cutlery as her she went berserk, bending and breaking it all until it was unrecognisable. There must have been literally thousands of pounds worth of damage.

She wasn't finished yet though. She found her husband's car parked outside and trashed that too. What do they say about a woman scorned?

Obviously with hindsight, I don't know if it was a good idea to tell her about her husband, but she insisted she was glad she found out and got it all out of her system. As her husband was a policeman he didn't want the whole story to come out so the whole incident was played down and hushed up. She got away with it all! He chose to keep quiet as he had become the laughing stock of the station.

I look back on this and I smile, but there was a lot of damage caused. I didn't really go looking for this; she came to ask my advice, and afterwards we often laughed about it. She moved on and is now happily married to a new man.

There was another lady who worked at Bodgers: she

worked on the Estee Lauder make-up counter. She was a similar age to me, and she had a grown-up son. She was always talking about his struggling career, as he was a budding young actor.

One day she approached me.

"Can't you give my boy some advice?"

"I don't know him

"If he comes in would you see him?"

"Well not in the shop I was beginning to get a bad reputation. The bosses didn't like my stories and I was always being told by them, "Don't do this in the store!"

"Look", I said "There is no way I can talk to him in the store and I'm really very busy, so where will I find him?"

"I'll make arrangements and get him to take you for a pub lunch and you can talk to him there

"Okay", I said.

It was arranged for a couple of weeks later and I met this tall, young man. He was very pleasant, but very nervous. We sat in the pub and started to chat.

His name was Rene, but it wasn't just the acting he was worried about; he was very upset about his ongoing romance. His girlfriend was moving in very different circles. She was also in the acting profession and was meeting well known stars. (As it worked out, she left him, and went off with somebody who is a very well known television actor whom she eventually married).

I started to tell Rene about his forthcoming career. I told him he would be in films and I would see him on television.

"Are you sure?" he said.

"Oh yes. You have a very bright future. One of the films you will be in has a connection to India. I keep seeing a very bright stone. I don't know if it is a diamond or a sapphire; I don't know exactly what it is, but I feel it's quite a long exciting film

I told him I could also see him being in Emmerdale, the television soap, playing a solicitor.

"Not very likely" he said. He was still very anxious about his girlfriend.

"I'm awfully sorry, but she won't be staying with you

"It's probably because I'm only a struggling actor You can't make people fall in love or stay together. He was terribly sad and not really paying a great deal of attention to his career, his mind clearly on other things.

Lunchtime was over and I had to go back to work. He was quite reluctant for me to go but I told him,

"Wait and see what happens and then perhaps I'll see you on another occasion

As it turned out, Rene did make an Indian epic called the "Star of India" which he had a large role in. Also, he appeared in Emmerdale as a solicitor, as I had told him.

He came back to see me. This time we went more in depth about his life. He said he was very keen to return to India.

"Be very careful if you go back, I think you may suffer with very poor health

"No, I'm very fit", he replied confidently, but this was a worry to me.

I also told him I could see him in a huge car, either a Jaguar

Paul, adult cot death

SOCCER manager Terry Venables was on the ball when asked to help boost a charity draw — he donated a football signed by his entire Barcelona team.

It will be just the ticket as a prize during an event to raise money for Great Ormond Street Hospital for children.

El Tel on ball with help for young patients

Me with football given by Terry Venables
December 11 1986

Missing James Harmon

Colin Colgate, Bills best friend

Roxanne and Bill

Holiday cottage opposite grave-yard where I saw Linda Barrett

Church-yard where I saw spirit of Linda Barrett

Victoria the Bridesmaid with Cousins Robert and Gareth

Air Historical Branch (RAF)
MINISTRY OF DEFENCE Room 411
Lacon House Theobalds Road London WC1X 8RY

Telephone (Direct Dialling) 01-430 - 6155
(Switchboard) 01-430 5555

Mrs S Willcox
120 Otley Drive
Gants Hill
Ilford
Essex   IG2 6NF

Your reference

Our reference
D/AHB(RAF)8/27
Date

11 June 1984

Dear Mrs Willcox

I refer to your letter of 23 May 1984 in which you enquire about two RAF casualties
Ronald Charles Jackson and Dennis Watson.

I have traced a Ronald Charles Jackson, of RAF Kai Tak, who was taken prisoner by
the Japanese when Hong Kong fell on Christmas Day 1941. He died whilst a prisoner of
war on or about 28 December 1943.

On Dennis Watson it is more difficult; there are at least two Dennis Watsons, and
several more Dennis Watsons with other middle names. I cannot therefore identify
with certainty this man.

I regret I cannot be of greater assistance than this.

Yours sincerely

E. A. Munday.

E A MUNDAY
Air Historical Branch 5 (RAF)

M.O.D Letter

Spirit boy photo taken by me outside Beatrix Potter's home Lake District

Photo of me, night I met Robert Plant Led Zeppilin

Dominique (Mile End)

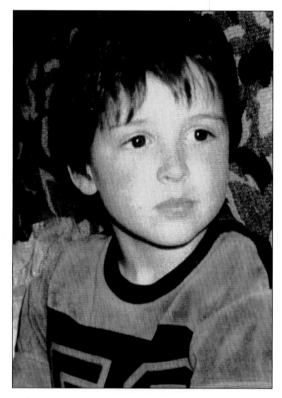

My little grandson James

or Rolls Royce. He was going to make a lot of money from his acting. Things were very much on the up. He laughed. He was still struggling, living in a small flat, doing odd jobs in between acting and sometimes staying with his mother. I said I didn't feel he was going to be totally famous, but I felt a very good living was to be made through his acting.

I saw him a couple of years later. He turned up on my doorstep one day in the most beautiful pale blue Jaguar car he had bought with all his acting money.

"Let me take you for a spin", he said. I climbed in and we drove around the local streets. He started telling me about a lot of the predictions that had come true.

He had just come back from India and whilst there he had caught Malaria. He was travelling on his own, and was wondering around when he passed out. He had become extremely ill. Had it not been for some villagers who found him and took him into a mud hut, bathed him, nursed and looked after him he would have died. Rene said he had no idea he could become so ill and how lucky he felt to have survived. I believe he made several donations to the poverty-stricken people of the village that had saved his life.

There was also another girl who worked on the Estee Lauder make-up counter in Bodgers. She was tall, very beautiful, almost regal. I think she was my favourite person in the store.

She was going out with a handsome Greek boy. He was serving in the RAF so she didn't see an awful lot of him, but every moment that she could she would pop over to Greece to be with him and when he came over to England he would stay with her. She was desperately in love with him and was saving and buying all sorts of things for their future home. She would ship out the items she had bought all the way to Greece.

On one occasion I started to talk to her in a very strange voice.

"Shirley, you're talking Greek!"

"I can't be. I don't know any Greek

"Yes you are!"

I started talking about her boyfriend's mother.

"Oh my god. That's her to a tee!"

I named all of her boyfriend's family: the father, brothers, grandparents. I said all of the names yet I had no idea of how Greek pronunciation sounded or knew anything about foreign languages. But I did know this lady who was coming through so strongly had died, so in her lunch break the girl hurried off to phone her boyfriend.

She found out that her boyfriend's mother had died and this was the spirit that was with me telling me things.

Speaking to this girl I described a house in Greece. Inside the house in a small room I saw a very deep window sill, and in the middle of the sill I could see a Dresden figure, a very beautiful figure of a young girl. The mother of the boyfriend was showing me all this and told me she wanted her son's girlfriend to have it because it was very similar to her, a beautiful English girl.

"I remember that. She always said to me 'I want you to have it'. How could you possibly know this, Shirley?"

The strangest thing was that for three days and four

nights I spoke Greek! I picked up the mannerisms of this woman; this spirit didn't leave me and I was getting quite scared. It was all very well giving readings for fun, but I hadn't taken this seriously and protected myself. It took me a long while to exorcise this spirit from me. She was an extremely strong woman and she hadn't wanted to die, and so had immediately entered me. It was an enormously scary thing that had happened to me and from then on I ensured that I better protected myself from the spirit world.

Another girl worked on the wig counter. She was really nice. She was Irish and a very happy, smiley character.

I used to look at her and I kept seeing a baby in her arms. One day I popped over to her and I asked if she was trying for a baby. Suddenly she was in floods of tears - I often had this awful effect on people. She told me she had tried for eleven years to get pregnant and she hadn't had any luck.

"Don't worry, you'll get pregnant in August. Are you going to Devon on holiday?" I said.

"Oh my god", she said, "that's where we are going for our summer holiday!"

By October she was back at work, walking around with a huge smile on her face, looking like the cat that got the cream. Baby was in its way. I told her she was going to have a baby boy. I can't remember the date, but apparently it was the exact date I told her he would be born.

I saw her baby. He weighed 9lb 4oz and she gave me a wonderful surprise; she asked me if I would like to be his Godmother. She was Catholic and I am not. To go down that road in their religion just isn't me. I thanked her; it was the only time anyone had ever asked me to be godparent, and I was hugely flattered, but it felt wrong as our religions are so different. As I'm a spiritualist, it just wouldn't have worked.

40

Baby (Pink Dress)

Two sisters were friends of my youngest daughter.
Living in the same house for almost 40 years we got to know everyone: all the children, all their parents at the school gates, everybody in the same community.

One day one of the sisters came to my home. They were both blonde, beautiful and each married with a son and daughter. Tragedy had just hit their home. The younger sister had had a baby daughter that had just died. It was through negligence at the hospital. The older sister asked me to see her younger sister. She said she needed help and couldn't accept her baby was gone.

"Of course I'll see her", I told the sister. "I will try my best to give her spiritual guidance and evidence

She came to see me that evening. She was cold, nasty and obviously very upset. I excused all this as she had just lost her child.

The tiny little spirit came through and told me lots of things with great difficulty and passed message after message to her mum, yet she remained aloof and hostile.

After two hours I was exhausted and drained. I'd had

enough.

"We must finish now", I said.

"I hope you're not expecting me to pay you for talking to my own daughter? Why can you see her and not me? Surely she knows I'M her mother?"

I felt hurt and humiliated. I've never been in this for the money. If people have given small donations they have been put to good charitable use. I know she had suffered, but she didn't have to be so rude to me.

The little child had been due to be a bridesmaid with her cousin at another friends wedding. It was going to be a beautiful white wedding, but of course the little girl had gone and she wouldn't be wearing the dress, so they handed it over to the mother.

Several months later I was awoken by silk being rustled. I sat up in bed startled. I could see a small pink dress; it was swinging on a hanger from a picture rail. It was swinging fast, it couldn't have been the wind or rustling on its own. Then I saw the tiny little girl who should have worn the dress. She smiled and chuckled and told me,

"Mummy is going to have a new baby and it's going to be a girl", she laughed and then she was gone.

Oh god, I thought. How was I going to tell her Mum? I didn't feel at all inclined to phone her - I didn't even want to see her. But I am not mean, and I really do go out of my way to pass on messages. If the spirit has gone to the trouble to tell me something, I feel it's only fair to pass on the message. I decided to phone her sister.

"I've got some news - your sister is pregnant", I said.

The sister was shocked, but I continued.

"The baby who passed has been to my home and told me the new baby will be a girl

"I don't think so Shirley. My sister is definitely not going to have any more children and I know for a fact she isn't trying for a baby

I persisted.

"I'm sure it's true. I saw the child clearly - she was swinging her little bridesmaid dress. She looked absolutely beautiful; she chuckled and then was gone

Having listened she decided to go round to her sister's with a pregnancy test. Her sister wasn't pleased and she said there was no way she could be pregnant, but after a lot of persuasion she decided to do the test, just to shut her sister up.

The test was positive. Yes, she was pregnant.

It was only after the result did the sister tell her that she had got a phone call from me with a message from her child.

The baby was born, safe and well. It was a girl.

Just previously before the baby was born, I had met the mother in Mothercare. She must have been about eight months pregnant and she just cut me dead, and gave me a terrible look. I was out with my family in the local park after she had the baby, and we came face to face, but she still ignored me.

I never did her any harm, and after all she was the one who came to me so her attitude to me was surprising. But I am happy she has another healthy child and was happy to speak to her charming little girl in spirit.

41

Alisha

A young girl turned up at my home. She was very agitated.

"Are you okay?" I asked her.

"Yes, I was just wondering what you could tell me", she replied.

"I'm picking up concern about a little girl and hospital", I told her. I wasn't picking up death, thank goodness. "I'm seeing a lovely little girl; she looks tiny, but there is such a shot of black hair!"

"Oh yes", her mum said, "I came to you a year ago, I'd been trying desperately for a baby, and you said, 'Just relax, you'll have a daughter and she will be gorgeous. But you must be prepared for mild ailments at the hospital.' This is why I've come back. She hasn't left hospital yet. She isn't gaining weight

I knew the hospital, it was only about a five or ten minute walk from my house.

"When are you going?" I asked.

"I'm going back there straight away. I wanted to pop in and see you first, see if you could shed any light on it all

"Would you allow me to give her healing", I said.

"Oh Shirley, would you?"

"Of course", I was happy to help this nice young mum.

I saw her out and about three hours later I went up to the hospital. I hurried in. I was quite familiar with the hospital, as I had visited it on many occasions. I had been in there as a child myself and all my three children at odd times had been in there too for small things.

I met the mum and walked over to the cot. Laying there was a gorgeous little bundle with the most striking hair. Her hair was jet black, silky and shiny and she had the sweetest face, but she was so tiny.

I put my hand above her head and as I did so I felt a sharp pain shoot up my spine; it was like a rod.

"This feels like a lumber punch", I said to her mum.

"She had one this morning", she told me.

Immediately I smiled, then said,

"She's fine. Everything's going to be fine. I promise you, I'm being told she'll leave hospital in two weeks The mother looked at me, I know she was anxious. She thanked me and I left.

The next day the mother phoned me. She'd had good news from the hospital; baby had put on half an ounce. Within two weeks she had gained enough weight and she left hospital. Back at home she started to thrive.

I heard from her mum about a year later. The little girl was fit and well and her mum had started her second pregnancy.

42
Air Hostess

A young lady had come to me. She was an airhostess from Aberdeen and was on a trip to London. Her friends had been to see me and booked her an appointment for her birthday.

We got into her reading quite quickly and I described two young men coming through who had both died on motorbikes.

"I don't know anyone who has died on a motorbike", she said.

I gave her their names but they didn't mean anything to her. Fair enough I thought.

"This is definite; you're going to move", I told her.

"We were thinking about it", she said.

"I can see a beautiful house. I can hear a very strong Scottish accent. They're talking very fast. The house begins with a K-E...I'm not sure what the rest is", I explained. "It's going to be outside Aberdeen. The house is on a corner, and there's a slight hill I went on to describe the house in great detail.

"It sounds lovely. I'll keep my options open", said the lady.

I was getting a very strong link to a helicopter.

"I know you're an airhostess, but you don't have anything to do with helicopters though do you?" I asked.

"My husband is a helicopter pilot. He goes backwards and forwards to the oil rigs", she smiled.

"Ah, that must be it

"Yes we have a wonderful life flying about, but we rarely see each other as we're both so busy. The plan to move was to try and get a bit more routine in our life. We need to be more settled

"There's a baby coming", I said.

"That is what I'd love", she said and not long after she left.

The next day two ladies came to see me. I started their readings when all of a sudden a spirit boy appeared. He was very prominent and it was another motorbike death. I felt he had just died and he was very, very anxious to talk to me.

All of a sudden the telephone rang. I don't normally answer calls during a reading as it spoils the sitting for people, but the two ladies both insisted I answer it as we had only just begun, which was very understanding of them.

I picked up the phone.

"Hello, it's me. Do you remember me from yesterday? The airhostess from Aberdeen?"

"Yes. Hello dear

"I was called home immediately after I left you yesterday. I got a call to say my cousin had been killed on a motorbike. All the family is gathered and in absolute pieces. The strangest part is the corner where he died is where two of his friends died too. They had been friends since they were about four years old. The two names you gave me yesterday are his friend's names. All three boys died at different times in the exact same spot. I can't believe it

It doesn't give me satisfaction to predict the death of such a young man, but it is some comfort to know he would be met in spirit by his friends. The three spirits were together.

About eighteen months later I received a phone call.

"Shirley, do you remember me?"

"You'll have to remind me, I'm afraid?"

"I'm the airhostess from Aberdeen

"Oh yes, I remember. The boys on the motorbikes", I said.

"Yes. I just thought I'd phone to give you an update. I've moved house to a place called Kinnear, just outside Aberdeen. It's beautiful, just as you described it in every detail. We had a little boy, just like you said, and I've got another on the way. You said my second would be a girl, so we'll have to wait and see

43

Compassionate Friends

A lady came to see me through Compassionate Friends. She was very assured and confident.

I took her upstairs and she asked me to hold a signet ring she had brought along. Whilst I was gazing at her I could also see a young man and a red car. He looked about twenty two, and he and kept pointing at the ring.

"There's a young man here with a red car and he keeps pointing at the ring. The ring belongs to him and I know that you bought it for his twenty first birthday", I said to the lady.

"Yes that's right", she confirmed.

"He is your son, and I know that you know he is very happy, contented and at peace

"Yes I know he's safe. But I was wondering if you could tell me anymore?" she asked.

I sat and waited and watched. The whole scene was played out in front of me. This young man had driven at ferocious speed. He had a habit of doing wheel spins. He was a very confident young man. There was a terrible crash and he had not been wearing his seat belt. Consequently he had been thrown through the window and then been hit by an oncoming car.

I relayed all that I had seen to the mother.

"No, you've made a mistake. My son didn't go through the windscreen. He died inside the car in a crash

"Wait a moment", I said, and watched as they replayed the accident to me. "I'm awfully sorry, but I'm not being shown anything different. There's a screech, he did travel at quite a speed you know

"He did like to drive fast, but that wasn't the cause of the crash at all", she said firmly.

"Well all I can see is that he hit something because of the speed he was going and he's gone through the windscreen

"No, no, no, I'm afraid you're totally wrong. But you were right about lots of other things like the ring, his name and the way you described him

After chatting about other various stuff she left. I was left feeling a bit confused as it had been so clear the way I had seen this accident played out before me.

About three days later I had a telephone call from this lady.

"Hello Shirley, I came to see you a few days ago about my son", said the voice on the end of the phone.

"Oh hi. How are you?" I said.

"Well, I had to phone and tell you something Shirley. When my boy passed I was too distraught to hear any details about the crash and my husband decided not to tell me exactly what had happened to protect me. When I told him what you described the other night he couldn't believe it as that is exactly what happened. He did go through the windscreen

It saddened me that this young man had lost his life, but I felt relieved to know that what I was seeing was correct and could provide proof to his family that he was still around. Even though I have accurately seen and predicted many things over the years, it still surprises me to have what I say validated. I guess there is a sceptic in all of us, even me.

44

West Ham

West Ham United football team was and still is my husband's favourite football team. The wife of one of the most prominent players used to come to my house quite often. Sadly he had passed away. On one of her visits I told her she would shortly be going to the USA, but it was very important that she should not go over the Bermuda Triangle.

"I have no plans to go over there", she said. "It's definitely not on the agenda

We continued talking, me relaying messages, discussing things that had come true since her last visit, chatting and drinking tea, then she left.

A couple of days later she phoned me.

"Shirley, you'll never guess what's happened. I've been asked to accompany someone, all expenses paid to the USA to help them look at property", she said.

"How wonderful", I said. "But please don't go over the Bermuda Triangle. I'm not being fanciful, but every time I mention it I get a shudder and go cold. It's definitely coming from spirit

"Okay, I don't expect we'll go anywhere near it, but I'll

keep it in mind

They set off on their journey. They had good seats, the nibbles and drinks were flowing and they were having a great time. Suddenly the pilot came over the tannoy to update them on the progress of their flight. He announced they would shortly be flying over the Bermuda Triangle. The lady grabbed the nearest hostess and demanded to know what the pilot meant.

"Do you mean we are actually going to fly over the Triangle?" she asked frantically.

"Yes Madam", replied the hostess.

In her own words, she then completely lost it! She flew into hysterics and insisted the plane take another route. Then she started exclaiming that a medium advised her under no circumstances to go near the Bermuda Triangle. She was getting more and more agitated, and whether it was to pacify her, or her conviction in making the cabin crew believe in psychic phenomenon, the pilot took the unprecedented decision to divert the plane. I can't imagine how she must have felt, with all the other passengers no doubt fuming and giving her looks of daggers at being diverted.

As the plane made its way to another airport, shortly before it landed a woman passenger was taken seriously ill. There were no doctors onboard the plane and her illness was life threatening. She was immediately taken to hospital as soon as the plane landed. Things then became clear.

"Shirley, they told me if I hadn't so unceremoniously diverted the plane, that lady would have died in mid-air. If we had taken the original route she would have been too

163

far away from a hospital. It was only because we landed at another airport that she survived

I was speechless, but it was only because of this lady's guts and determination that she managed to get the plane diverted.

"Honestly, I have never thrown such a wobbly in all my life! I'm embarrassed thinking about it now!" she giggled over the phone.

We laugh about it now and how crazy it must have looked to the other passengers, but I'm sure there is one passenger indebted and grateful to her hysterics.

45
Nurse (South Africa)

A nurse came to my door, I knew she was a nurse because she still had her uniform on, so I didn't need to use my psychic powers to know that. She had the most stunning, long, honey coloured hair that cascaded down her back. She had freckles to match and was small and petite. As she walked up my stairs I followed, her thick hair swung from side to side, swishing.

We sat down. The first thing I saw with her was that she was very ambitious, totally career-orientated and very clever.

"You're going up the career ladder very fast. Are you going for promotion?" I asked her.

"Yes, I'm taking exams now. I've got three directions I could go. I was wondering if you could point me in the right direction?" she said.

"Erm, actually no", I said. "I know you are very ambitious but I can't see you taking any of those paths. I'm seeing a total cut off

"No way! Nursing is my life. I love nursing", she exclaimed.

"What about marriage and children?" I asked her.

"Well yes I would like that, but not until later. Lots of

people leave it until later now anyway. I've got friends who haven't had children until their late thirties. I want to put all that on hold. My career comes first

I gave her my crystal ball to hold to help me with her reading. She was so determined about her career that I was doubting what I was being told. But as she handed me back the ball all I could see and hear was "She isn't going any further up the ladder It was all around her.

"Your destiny is going to change. It's nothing to do with illness or anything scary, in fact I think it's going to be a new chapter in your life and it will be wonderful. Have you ever thought of going to South Africa?" I asked her.

"No. Never. I don't know anybody there. I've never wanted to go there. The three job interviews I've got lined up are in the best London hospitals and I stand a very good chance of getting all three and I wanted you to help me decide which one to take

"Oh. South Africa is looming very strongly. Who's Jon?" I said.

"I don't know a Jon", she answered.

"I'm getting the name Jon. J-O-N. He looks nice, strong, sturdy, fit. Looks like he could run long distances. He's got dark, wavy hair and this healthy, outdoor complexion

"I work with a John who's a doctor, but he's quite skinny and willowy" she said.

"No. That's not him. This one is very much the outdoors type", I confidently said.

"Right. So, are you telling me I'm going to meet a man like this?" she asked hesitatingly.

"Yes. Definitely. South Africa is so strong. I KNOW you are going to go there. And this man is going to feature heavily in your life and he has a link with South Africa

We laughed and chatted about lots of other things for the rest of the reading.

Two weeks later I got a phone call.

"Shirley do you remember me? I came to see you a couple of weeks ago. I'm the nurse with the long hair", she explained.

"Yes of course. How are you?" I replied.

"Shirley, you are not going to believe what's happened. The day after I saw you I had a day off and went shopping in Oxford Street. I was rushing along as usual and barged into this bloke who was coming out a shop. He shouted at me "Steady! Steady!" as I pushed past him and I recognised it being a South African accent. I stopped and I looked. Then he said to me "Joanne? Is that you?" I suddenly recognised him. His name was Jon and he was a friend of my brother's from years ago. So I said, "What are you doing here?" and he said he was on holiday for a month. He moved to South Africa about 14 years ago, but grew up with my brother. We got chatting and I arranged for him to come to my mothers house so that we could have a get together and he could see my brother and his family, so I gave him my number

Joanne and Jon got together. She put her career on hold, married him and moved to South Africa. For someone who was so resolute and adamant, it's interesting to see how her destiny changed so radically.

46

Lake District (Spirit Boy)

Whenever we're away on holiday with the grandchildren, we always take them out on 'Mystery Tours'. We set off in about three cars, my husband leading, and I direct us all to somewhere special.

One year in the Lake District we found our way to Beatrix Potter's house. It's a beautiful old farmhouse near Windermere. It's been turned into a museum with all her original furniture, paintings and story books.

We went in with great excitement. There were quite a lot of other people visiting, wandering in and out of the rooms.

My granddaughter, who was about three years old, tugged at my sleeve.

"Look Nanny, there's a little boy and he's following us She pointed at a spirit boy. I had seen him too. He was just head and shoulders and was floating around. I kept glancing at other people, but nobody else seemed aware of him. He looked very old fashioned. His black hair was plastered down and his collar was rounded, no points.

We continued walking round and I decided to take some photos of the house. I got the family to gather around the door and I saw the boy spirit close to them. I took some photos of the family then after they moved away I took some photos of the spirit boy who was now in the nearby bushes. I decided to get them printed immediately, as my impatience was getting the better of me. I was keen to see whether the spirit had been captured on film.

We went to a chemist shop and they said they would print them within the hour. I waited in the shop for the whole hour, eager to get my hands on the photos. Once I had paid I started to thumb through the photos. I was thrilled; there he was, the spirit boy on about eight photos.

The next time I went to the Beatrix Potter house I showed the photos to the people who worked there. They confirmed they'd had many sightings of the boy before, but never a photo. I decided to take more photos of the house whilst I was there as I was very drawn to the house. I didn't see the spirit boy on that visit so didn't rush for the photos to be developed like before, but waited until I got home. When I got them back there was a very strong, psychic, blue light all around the porch where the boy had appeared before, but nothing quite as clear as the previous time. Spirits are very real and often appear in photos, but for me this felt extra special.

I often did services for spiritualist churches: this one was on a Thursday afternoon in Ilford. Prayers and hymns were part of the service, but I had to give an address and clairvoyance to as many as possible, every one wanted a message.

Today I decided to talk about my spirit photo I had taken at Beatrix Potters House.

While telling every one, I kept being drawn to the lady in the second row, on the end by the exit sign. A motor bike was revving up and a tall lad about 16 was astride the bike; he obviously was attached to the lady in beige coat.

I finished my talk and immediately started the clairvoyance.

"Andrew is next to you on his motor bike", I told her, "He has not been in spirit long, but he is fine and often at home with you. He also tells me he went to Beatrix Potter's house

"That's right" she said "we all went together the week before he died. " The motor bike he tells me was a present from you for his sixteenth birthday but he hardly had time to use it", I said.

"That's right he had only been on it half an hour and then he was killed The mother said

The reading in public can be very emotional, and more than once we all cried in unison.

Andrews mum Doreen, became a familiar face at every venue I appeared at.

She brought many people to see me and she also became a dear friend. She also had three wonderful daughters I got to know.

I send love to all the family; I have lost touch since my move.

I met another lady in the same church, Emma, whilst I was giving clairvoyance from the rostrum.

Her beautiful daughter Mary Ann had died in a car accident; so tragic. It was her cousin's birthday and a night out was planned for December 19th. Mary Ann had not wanted to go; she had split up with her boyfriend and just wanted to stay in. When the four friends called around Mary Ann had washed her hair and was in her dressing gown drying her hair.

"You must come out", they told her "it won't be the same without you

They went to town on her appearance, curling her hair, sorting out her clothes and waiting while she put on her make up. Thus finished the five friends went out and had an unforgettable night out. One girl was dropped off home, and minutes later the car swerved, hit an object and rolled over and over.

Mary Ann was killed outright; the other three had not a scratch.

Destiny is marked at birth.

The strange thing is, two weeks earlier Mary Ann had portrait photos done in a studio for her mum. She said she had a feeling she would not live long.

I met several of her relatives and the family was in touch with me for many years.

One of Mary Ann's brothers had tiny twin daughters and, at the age two, one of the twins was lost to spirit and I saw her together with Mary Ann.

A serene angel with a cherubic angel both at peace.

47
Hanged Uncle

The young woman was sitting nervously in my little room quietly dabbing the tears from her eyes. I had seen her before , and she was usually so bubbly with the most attractive Irish accent.

"Oh Shirley help me", she asked.

"I'll try", I said.

"Please take this It was a man's watch: I often held an article belonging to the sitter to help me tune in. I held the watch tightly waiting for a sign.

A vision was starting to come to me. Three men roughing up a lone male.

This was horrible – they had a rope and were tightening it around the sole male's neck

A vicious yank and it looked like his neck was broken.

This was not all – they strung him up to the rafters; this was done with enormous difficulty, and they went on to wreck the flat, smashing everything and chucking papers all over the place.

Cooking oil was poured everywhere and a match thrown on to the oil strewn papers and left. I was relaying all this to my sitter with great care.

"I knew it", she stated.

"The police said he committed suicide, but my uncle was the most wonderful person and devout Catholic. Shirley, Catholics don't do suicide well - very rarely, and definitely not him.

He had no enemies a good job and his life was fine He had absolutely no reason to kill him self."

I wanted more, and I patiently waited for the scene to reappear. The fire did not take off and burn. God only knows why but that is what happened. The police said he trashed his flat beforehand.

"I'm going back to the police I will not accept his suicide. Will you tell them for me all that you have seen?"

I promised I would, but police do not usually listen to mediums.

"I'm going back to his flat", she said. He loved it and was happy there. As mum and dad are his next of kin, it will go to them, but they can't bring them selves to go in there although they have the keys."

She thanked me and left.

She returned to me about a month later. I was astonished; apparently his neighbour had been away and had not known of her uncle's demise

"The morning it happened" he told her "he had heard lots of voices and thudding and all sorts of goings on in the flat. I rang the bell to give your uncle my key, but no one answered, so I left it down stairs with Mrs. Brown who said she would pass it on to your uncle, and I flew off to New York."

"Have you told the police all this" I asked him?

"No, no one has spoken to me but I know he would NEVER kill himself."

The police did re examine all this evidence the body was exhumed, and the neck was proven to be broken in such a way, it could not have happened by being hanged up.

The death certificate was changed to murder by persons unknown.

Much later three men were charged with the murder.

My young Irish friend was so happy she came to me for a reading.

48

Red Haired Actress

There was a knock. I opened the door to a stunning redhead. Yes, I knew her - I had seen her lots of times and also knew the family.

"Shirley I need your help Here we go again!

She was crying before I opened my mouth. Yes, I did have this effect on people, but tears so soon……..

On closer inspection she wasn't well.

"I must stay here, at least tonight. I feel dreadful"

"Come in love - do you want some tea?"

"No, I'd love a glass of water, and could you make me some toast with no butter - I am starving

My radar was working - she had to be pregnant.

I had told her a baby boy was going to come if she wasn't careful.

"Oh Shirley - why did I not take notice of what you warned me?"

"I did get the wonderful part in the theatre - it's my biggest part yet, I can't have another child; it would spoil everything

She was a real beauty, with natural deep red hair (not ginger) and soft wavy curls cascading down her back. Her skin was fragile and ethereal. This was a highly educated young woman who went to RADA. Mother was a choreographer and accomplished dancer; father a doctor.

The last baby, a girl had been fostered. This I had predicted three years ago. "My mother will kill me if she finds out I'm pregnant again. You must let me go to the doctor - you know the one you sent Justine to

"Justine was not registered with any doctor and she was over from Australia.

Please do not ask me to help you get an abortion. I will not participate - it must be your choice" I stated. "What about your parents do they know you have come to me?"

"Oh Shirley please phone them, mum and dad love and trust you. Tell them I'm just staying one night and tell them I'm in the shower

Duly done, I sorted out the sheets for her hopefully short stay

The baby was flushed away. The actress returned blooming to conquer her audiences.

Why, why, why, we have to wonder, do some girls have such heart break trying to conceive, and such pain in their loss with miscarriage, ectopic, even still-birth and attempts with I V F treatment.

Another of the questions we can not answer.

49

Two Tonies

A lady came to my home. As soon as she entered my little room, a young boy started talking to me: he had been run over by a lorry.

He was playing with his friends hitching rides on the back of these very large vehicles.

When a lorry was almost stationery, the boys would hop on to a ridge and hang on to the back, and as soon as it started to speed downhill they would jump off. Young Tony was crushed by a second lorry.

There was another Tony too - young Tony's uncle, also killed by a lorry on his push bike. The two spirits had never met on earth but were together and safe in the spirit world. Such a sad loss for one family.

50
Caren

Spirits are very good at predictions about babies.

Caren, a lovely girl from Manchester, desperately wanted a baby, but after five attempts at I V F she and her husband were running out of funds and hope.

"You must do it one more time; you will definitely have a gorgeous little boy

"My husband has said there is it no more money to be wasted.

Caren and I chatted for a long time; the spirits were so right about all aspects of her life that they couldn't be wrong about a baby.

A few days later a male came for a reading. His life was very colourful - there were lots of Romanies in his aura: high rounded horse-drawn caravans, and the spirit of an old Romany lady with black hair, gold hooped earrings and piercing black eyes.

"Tell him he will have a son, the image of him little David

The man looked at me sharply

"That's why I have come. She was my grandmother, I always loved her and saw her spirit at her funeral. You saw my wife a week ago and told her we should have one more attempt at IVF. We will try once more for a baby.

He hugged and kissed me and was gone.

10 months later little David was born.

I still get a photo of him every Christmas.

I love these happy endings.

51

Girl (car crash)

A very chilling story was told to me one Sunday morning. I opened the door to a young lady. She was about twenty five. She smiled nervously, and as I went to shut the door she hesitated.

"Are you afraid?" I asked her.

"Yes", she replied.

"There's no need to be, I'm not going to hurt you. You look familiar. Have you been here before?" I enquired.

"Yes, I came a year ago

"You don't have to stay. I won't be at all offended if you'd prefer to leave", I assured her.

"No I want to stay, but I'm scared", she said looking apprehensive.

"I promise I won't tell you anything scary", I told her. "If you want to stay, go and make yourself comfy upstairs and I'll bring you a cup of tea. But if you would feel more comfortable going, please don't let me stop you

"No, I'll stay, but I don't want any tea", she said and began climbing the stairs.

I immediately noticed there was a girl spirit with us. She was beautiful; slim with long blonde hair.

"You do realise there's a girl here with us", I gently told her.

"Oh, I wondered if you would mention her", she said.

"Don't be afraid, she looks fine. She's stunning. She's about twenty three, slender, with long blonde hair", I explained. "Hold on, she's telling me how she passed." I listened to the spirit. "She was with a young man in a metallic silver car. There was a terrible screech, crunch and crash. The car rolled over and over. She's clutching the back of her head. She died instantly."

The girl looked at me then spoke.

"When I came here a year ago I came here with her. You kept telling us that you could see a horrible car accident that worried you and you kept holding your head. That's why I was scared to come back. But since she died all the other things you have told me have come true. You told me loads of things. You said I would meet a nice man called Lee and he'd be a steady influence on my life. Well, I have and he is", she smiled.

I tried my best to explain to her that our destinies are mapped. We don't have control over when we're going to go.

"I understand all that, but it doesn't make it any easier to figure out why someone so special should go?" she asked.

It was a question I had asked and failed to get an answer for many, many times over the years. I had encountered so many instances of vivacious, successful, beautiful, intelligent, kind souls being taken and have only ever reached the conclusion that only God knows why they must go.

"I'm glad I came", the girl said to me. "I feel I've put something to rest."

52

Pakistani Girl

It has always been wonderful when a life that has been unfolded to me over the years all comes true – with total proof.

A young frightened girl came to my home in Gants hill; it must be fourteen years ago. She had beautiful large expressive brown eyes brimming with tears and sadness. I'm not gentle - I suppose a little brusque: it comes out straight to the point, and I tell the total truth.

"Your husband does not respect you - he is brutal, mean and makes your life hell. You must leave this marriage; it is blocking your whole future. There is a little boy. Take him with you and protect him - he will be clever."

She cried and cried. She knew all about this, but I suppose people with problems need a stranger to put it in perspective.

Words are easily said; I know this, the easy way out is to stay. Where do you go with a small eighteen month old child - no money, no relatives. This young lady was from Karachi; a Pakistani girl married to an Irish Catholic – not an easy combination.

She 'phoned and visited me often. She was bright, hard

working and ambitious.

"You should go to college" I told her. "I can see you studying law - you will pass your exams and get your degree. You must learn to drive - I can see you with your own car

These all seemed easy words. She hadn't left her husband yet, but she said it helped her to keep coming to see me, as what I had seen for her dad and mum and other family members came exactly true.

Time passed and my Pakistani friend returned. She had her own, gold-coloured car now, had left her husband and was renting a house with her small son and a lodger.

She also was attending college; she was on her way to study law. I saw her many times and encouraged her to keep studying. It paid off as she got her degree in law and also her divorce.

Her life was so extreme that one day I told her she must write a book. Her cruel husband was a twin. The other twin had unfortunately died aged twenty one in a car accident. He used to come through to give her guidance; He was her guardian angel.

This is proof that when her life was nothing but struggle and hardship the spirit always came to her.

I would often remind her to keep at her book; it is now published and on sale in many continents.

I'm very proud of my Pakistani friend; her life is on the up.

53
Karen

Every time I went into my little room I saw the same girl, nineteen or twenty years old, with blond curls, and smiling. I knew she had been brutally killed, but I also thought she looked familiar.

About three weeks later I was reading my local paper when I saw her 'photo and write- up: it was my eldest daughter's young school friend.

She had been in our home countless times and played as a tiny child with my children upstairs in the small room. Oh dear - her poor mother; this was her only child, nineteen years old and stabbed to death by a woman.

I must phone her.

We talked and talked, but I did not mention seeing her daughter's spirit. She had been missing for weeks and when she had first appeared I could not put a name to her face as I had not seen her for at least eight years.

"Thank you for speaking to me", she said "most people hurry away"

"I know", I said. It is difficult for a lot of people to deal with grief.

The years dwindled by and the mother always reminded

me how lucky I was to have three married children and grandchildren.

"When I watch Roxanne I think my daughter would have had children just like she has".

She is right to remind me I do count my blessings.

54

Three Dead Christmas Day

It was January, and my husband and I were going to King's Lynn to the sales. I rush around the shops with glee, while he sits in the car reading the paper.

The day was freezing; I had a flask of coffee in the boot in case I was ages. I was happy - I just love shopping.

We were on the A47 road nearing King's Lynn when I noticed a pretty girl at the road- side. She had no coat, a short skirt, tiny vest and hair blowing in the wind. She waved.

"Oh my god, we must stop and give her a lift - she must be freezing".

"What are you talking about?" my husband said.

"That girl".

"There is no girl", he replied.

"Oh" - she had vanished.

"You are quite mad", he said "you must never drive with the things you see".

I knew I had seen her; she was lovely - only about seventeen years old.

I had fun at the shops; bargains are worth rummaging for!

I returned to the car and we drank a cup of coffee by

the harbour, with a nice bun I had bought from Marks and Sparks. Content, I said "I'm ready for home".

On the opposite side of the road on the return journey, at about the same spot as I had seen the girl, just off the road, were three small wooden crosses with lots of flowers. I wondered if she was one of the spirits linked to the crosses.

About a year went by a man and a lady came to my home to have a reading. As soon as they sat down the young girl I had seen all those months ago by the road side was in my room, and the atmosphere was freezing and strange.

This couple were the parents of the girl and one of the boys. It happened on Christmas day. A terrible accident: three lovely young people brother/sister/best friend.

What a tragic loss.

55
Exorcism (School Kids)

I t was about ten o clock on a Friday evening when I heard a loud knocking on my door. I was surprised to see the police. They wanted me to go to a house where a group of children had been playing with a ouija board, and it had all gone terribly wrong. The kids were fifteen, sixteen, possibly 17 years.

The so-called fun had started in a large house, with the parents out for the evening.

At first I thought they were drugged; such wild-eyed screaming terror. A policeman escorted me in and said he would stay with me. The three others were trying to contact the parents of the children. Only one girl seemed okay.. She was trying to pacify some of the group - twelve in all.

"Mark has locked himself in the bedroom at the front of the house!" one screamed. "He said he is going to jump",

Oh my god what on earth had been happening.

The perfume and mist of joss sticks was burning, and several candles gave an eerie light around the room. I took control. "Would you all sit quietly for me please", I said. "I am a spiritualist medium". I held out my cross. "If we could all hold hands and sit in a circle".

Fortunately the table they had in the middle of the room was round with several chairs around it.

Two boys were thumping on the upstairs bedroom door calling for Mark. Another lad was lying still on the lounge floor, eyes large and staring, another wondering helplessly back and forth the length of the lounge. "Sit still, hold hands, and we will say the Lord's Prayer", I told them.

Three more policemen burst in. "Stay quiet", I asked my group. The police, noticing us, quietly moved into the hall.

My attention was back to my group of children.

"I will ask for a cloak of protection for us all", I said "and ask for all spirits you have contacted tonight to leave". This was having a good effect.

"Not one spirit will enter you, or stay with you", I said. Three of the girls started to cry, two boys were a quivering mess, the other two quite rational "Keep holding hands", I told them "and the energy you collected will recede".

"We have a young spirit here who I believe you all knew: he says he is safe and in a good place. He I believe is who you were trying to contact. He died from sniffing a substance".

"Yes, yes" they said – "he was in our class".

"He died just before last Christmas".

"We so wanted to contact", him they said.

"Did any of you see anything?" I asked.

"No".

"I have been a medium for many years. I am the seventh child; this often enables spirits to get through more easily. "Your friend is Lee?" I asked.

"Yes" they murmured.

"Please don't be afraid ask me anything".

"Could one of your officers get us some water and eight glasses?"

"Sip slowly", I told them as I poured and filled the glasses.

All the youths were quiet and steady. "Would any of you like to tell me if you are afraid and uneasy?" They were beginning to look sheepish.

"I don't really think it is a good idea to play with a ouija board", I stated.

They were all saying "no", they would NEVER touch one again.

A loud door slammed it was a car, high heels tapping into the house

"Who are you, how dare you come in to my home, what is going on?" she blazed at me.

Before I could open my mouth two police officers hurriedly took her into the hall.

I wasn't ready to rush off - I wanted to sort out the others; my little group at the table were fine now. Mark was still on the window sill: a doctor, nurse, and the police were trying to get him in, but they would not let me near to him.

The owner of the home, the woman who had screamed, at me was told I had saved and calmed the situation at the police invitation.

One of the officers took me home.

The use of the ouija board is up to the individual, I would not recommend it.

56
Led Zeppelin – Robert Plant

I worked as a cashier in Bejams, (now known as Iceland) the frozen food shop. It was a very happy job; local, the girls were fun, the boss a very fair and good person to work with who really looked after us all.

As I was senior in age to everyone (the boss was only about thirty and all the other staff were on their early twenties), I was referred to as "Mother". When the young girls had an emotional problem the boss would ask me to take them up to the staff room, make them a cup of tea, and sort out their relationships. What a doddle! And they paid me a wage!

At Christmas or birthdays the boss would call upon me to act as chaperone at the various parties.

"Please go along with the girls, Mother. You can keep an eye on them and a night out would do you good", he'd say to me. We all had hysterics behind his back. Those girls were wild and could teach him a thing or two.

It was Jackie's birthday - she was nineteen. She had no boyfriend, but she had her eye on someone and was ready to pounce.

"We're going to the Seven Kings Hotel", she ordered. " 'He' will be there and, Shirley, perhaps you can give him the-once-over and give me a few hints to help get him!" I laughed at her scheming.

The Seven Kings hotel was a large impressive building set back from the road, close to the train station. I loved the building: it was covered in Virginia Creeper and looked magnificent in the autumn. It was often used for music gigs and up-and-coming bands would play there. (It is sadly demolished now).

Fourteen of us were meeting there. My husband was at home with my three kids. I got dressed up, did my hair and make-up and then off I went.

Lots of people were jammed inside. The music blared out and the singer was loud. The place was alive with swaying bodies, clapping hands. We drank, we danced and Jackie and I moved in on her chosen bait. I pulled him onto the dance floor and he danced along with Jackie and me, then his friend joined us.

After a while I grabbed another one of the girls to dance with Jackie and excused myself for a sit down. It was a wonderful, happy evening. I enjoyed watching the dancing and the birthday girl was having a ball.

"May I sit here?" I looked up. A tall, colourful, large man was looking at me.

"Yes. Be my guest".

The chairs were close, but he was not watching the dancing; I felt him studying me. I thought it was time I made a move to go and started to get up.

"Please don't go", he said. "May I get you a drink?"

I looked fully at him.

"You look familiar", racking my brain from where I'd seen his face before.

"I'm in the band that was just on. I was singing, but I wanted a breather. I was watching you. You are very different to everyone else. You don't really fit in here".

"Oh charming!" I was on the defensive. "Are you suggesting I'm too old to be here?"

"No. I'm so sorry. I didn't mean to offend you. I just wanted to talk to you. It was nice to think not only do the young, mad lot come to hear us, but people like you do too. Oh god, does that sound vain?"

"People like me? Listen matey, I haven't a clue who you are or what music you play. And to be perfectly honest, I didn't like it anyway. I'm only here because the girls at work dragged me along. I happen to be married with a husband and three lovely children at home".

He started to laugh. "I like you, you're honest!" He laughed and shrugged his shoulders. "You don't like my music. Fair enough!"

"I'm sorry, but it's loud and not at all me", I told him. He was very nice actually, had good manners and was very polite. I may have been a bit too quick in snapping at him.

There was a commotion around us and his band members appeared to tell him, in no uncertain terms, to get back on the stage and continue the gig.

"No, I'm staying here with my friend", he told them.

"Who the hell is she?", yelled one of the boys from the band.

Ignoring his band he grabbed me by the arm and led me

to the bar.

"What's your name?" he asked.

"I'm Shirley. And you are?"

"Well our band's called Led Zeppelin – I'm Robert Plant". It didn't mean a thing.

The girls were swarming around.

"Do you two know each other?" one girl demanded.

"How did you land him?" asked another.

"I don't know what you're talking about", I said. "He only plays music with those others.

It felt like a cat fight was erupting around me. I had never been into the music scene. I had gone out to work aged fourteen, married young, had my children. This was not a familiar environment for me. I wanted to leave; I was beginning to feel uncomfortable. I saw my friends from work.

"Jackie, I'm going to get a cab home".

"No you're not", said the musician, "I'll take you".

"No. You can't", I said.

"Yes I can and I will. Please, finish your drink and then we'll leave".

The rest of the band were not happy, but their singer refused to perform and there was nothing they could do about it. We went outside.

He wouldn't hear of me calling a cab and showed me to his car. It was the biggest, most elaborate car I have ever been in. Inside the whole front was lit with gadgets and buttons. I told him I like Diana Ross and she was soon singing in the background.

"My son would go mad if he could see this", I told him.

"Let's go and take him for a ride", he offered.

"No. Best not, he'll be fast asleep tucked up in bed".

I don't know how, but the psychic bit always comes up.

I told him about a friend of his who had died in very sad circumstances. The boy gave his name. The musician was bereft; he had only passed in the last couple of months and the death had affected him badly.

"The music I was playing tonight was for him. I felt his presence up there. That's when I came over to you".

He drove me to my home and we sat in his car and talked for hours. He wouldn't come in for a cup of tea - he said it would be intrusive. My husband had come out to see what was going on and I told him I needed to talk to this man. He understood it was to do with spirits and went back to bed.

I have met over the years hundreds of wonderful people from all walks of life, including lots in the media too, but he was one of the nicest people I've met in my life.

I remember telling him he'd be famous and have a big comeback in later years. He offered me the chance to go to his concerts, but I never took up his offer.

I would like to pay tribute to a gentleman and gifted musician.

57
Leslie Flint

When we used to visit Leslie Flint for direct voice séances, Ellen Terry and Isadora Duncan spoke to us: both ladies said they had visited my home.

I know for certain that Isadora had when I was young - ten or twelve years old she; came through my bedroom wall.

I have also seen a vision on numerous occasions when a large black car would be parked on a cliff. The occupants were a tiny boy and small girl accompanied by a young woman.

The vision never changed, the car would slowly roll towards the edge of the cliff and fall several feet before crashing down. Always a man in a chauffeur uniform would appear at the top of the cliff.

After researching Ellen Terry's life and visiting her beautiful home in the Kent countryside, I found out the two children killed with their nanny were in fact Ellen Terry's grand children - their mother was Isadora Duncan, and she was co-habiting with Ellen Terry's son. He, however, was married and had several children with his wife.

The very sad twist to all this was, Isadora Duncan was strangled by the long scarf she always wore. It got tangled in the wheels of a sports car she was in: this was the lady I saw coming through my bedroom wall.

58

Honda Car

Ayoung woman came to see me. I'd seen her a couple of times before. She was young, bubbly and excitedly happy.

"Shirley, you were right. My dream has come true!" Her dream was in the shape of a Honda car and her husband had bought it for her birthday as a surprise.

"Last reading you told me I'd get one!" she gushed excitedly.

I felt something was wrong. I wasn't happy about the car.

"Is it new?" I inquired.

"Yeah, yeah brand new. Only four months old. The owner was a car fanatic who changes his motor as often as his socks!"

"No". My instinct was telling me something was up. I was restless and scared. Something was telling me things weren't right. "You can't drive this car. There will be a terrible accident if you do. There will be fire, it will blow and burn

The woman was mortified. I didn't want to ruin her joy of having this new car, but at the end of the day her safety was more important, and my intuition was telling me this car was anything but safe.

"Please stop Shirley. I love it and I've waited years to get it",

"Does 'cut and shut' mean anything to you?" I asked.

"I've heard the saying, but what do you mean?" she said.

"Look I don't know exactly, it's the message I'm getting, but I won't let you drive those beautiful kids home in it". She had two little girls and a small boy.

She still looked unconvinced.

"Be honest, would I try and deceive you?" I reasoned. "Or spoil your wonderful birthday present?" Have you smelt a rotting smell like bad eggs or rotting meat? Have you ever smelt it in the car?"

"That's strange", she answered, "I have actually, but only when I've been in the car. It's weird because it's an all-leather interior and new".

"The smell is spirit, giving you a warning. It's your grandmother 'Rachel'. She adores you and the kids and wouldn't hurt a hair on their heads. Have I ever told you anything that's not true?"

"Everything you've told me was true. And that smell, I've never smelt anything like it before and only ever smelt it in the car".

"Are you with a breakdown service?" I asked.

"Yes", she said.

"Right, 'phone them now and 'phone your husband too. There is no way you can drive home. I'm glad my husband isn't home; he'd say I was mad to think that this car isn't right", I confessed.

The AA came immediately. The car was examined…and

the police were called!

We watched as petrol drained out of it. A large low-loader was sent to collect it and taken away. We were told it was the most dangerous vehicle they had seen in a very long time. It could have gone up in flames at any moment.

It had been a very busy evening in my house!

The person who sold the car was taken to court and his business closed. Apparently this was not his first 'cut and shut'. He sustained a massive fine and a stay at Her Majesty's pleasure.

The story hit 'The News of the World' and we were both glad that she came to see me.

59
Bully Husband

One of the saddest readings I have ever given: a nice refined young woman was with me.

"Are you pregnant" I asked "I hope not", she said. "The two boys are enough; I love them and life would not be easy with three".

"There is a baby", I said. "It's a girl". But before I could stop it was out of my mouth –

"Your husband hits you doesn't he?

"Not always - not so much now; he doesn't like small children", she said.

My blood was up. "I hope he doesn't hit the kids?" I asked. This was a spiteful man, brutal.

"Oh I should not have come" she said. "Please don't dare say anything", she said. "He comes here for readings - he is very spiritual".

"Is he indeed?" Nothing makes me more angry than a bully. I won't see him again, let alone say anything. Please be very careful", I told her as she left.

About five months later she came back. Swollen belly and black rings around her eyes: she said it was tiredness, not the bully!

His bruises were hidden on her body, ribcage forearms and back. I made her show me.

"You must leave him", I implored. I don't usually give this type of advice but DANGER was all around her. Her dad, who had died in a car smash, was screaming abuse about him. His spirit was not at peace, and he said he would like to kill him.

All I kept seeing was this lovely pregnant girl being hurled down the stairs.

"Think of this baby and your boys", I begged.

"Go and stay with your mum - I know she would have you, or you can all come and stay here with me". I was so scared for her.

Her friend came to tell me she was found at the bottom of the stairs; she had lost the baby and had almost haemorrhaged to death- she was still in hospital.

About seven months later the hateful husband was severely injured in a car accident: paralysed from the neck downwards and confined to a wheelchair for life. The wife and children did not return to him - after her release from hospital, they went to stay with their grand mother.

What is that saying? God pays debts without money. Or what goes around comes around.

60
Girl Abused

Mediums have their uses. Where does a young girl go when she has a secret? A secret so awful she can't tell a teacher, a family friend, the family doctor and no way her mother?

This young lady was just sixteen- I don't see people any younger because I don't know what I may come out with and also it can be a lot to take in.

She was fidgety and nervous, twisting her hanky into a tight screwed-up mess. She licked her lips incessantly and kept pulling her skirt down to her calves.

"Who sent you here?" I asked.

"My friend told me her mum comes to see you".

"Please don't be scared of me. I've got daughters and grandchildren", I reassured her. "Would you like a cold drink?"

"Yes please. I don't mind what", she said.

I popped down to the fridge.

"It's nice and cold", I said as I handed her the can of Cola. "Now just try and relax".

I explained to her how I worked. I told her spirits came through to me and gave guidance, advice and protection to loved ones on earth.

"Your Nanny Elizabeth is here. She adored you. She tells me you had measles when you were six and she stayed to look after you. She was your dad's mum and he went to Canada after your mother and father divorced".

"That's right", she said.

I took a deep breath with what I was about to say and tentatively began.

"I know what is going on at home. Your stepfather is abusing you".

She started to cry uncontrollably.

"I hate him! He hurts me and threatens me", she sobbed.

This sort of thing makes my blood boil.

"Where is your mother when all this is going on?"

"At work", she replied. "He works at night in an orchestra and my mother doesn't get home until 6.30pm. He collects me and my little sister from school so we can do our homework and have tea before mum gets home. This is when he does things".

I couldn't begin to understand what this young girl was going through. It broke my heart to listen to it all.

"I have told my mother he does things, but she said I tell lies and he is good for all of us".

I leant forward and looked her straight in the eyes.

"Don't worry dear. It stops now-today. Your mother, where does she work? Do you have the number? Who else is there in the family?"

"There's my other Nan", she said.

"Do you like her? Does she know? Does she live close?" I fired at her.

"I love my Nan but she doesn't visit very often now because she doesn't like my step- dad and mum always takes his side".

I was ready to 'phone the police. I was the only person who had listened to her and I was not going to let her down. She desperately needed help.

"I think it would be best if I phoned your Nan and you can go home with her. I'll deal with your mother. And I promise he will never touch you again".

Her grandmother got a taxi and came immediately. She was distraught.

"Why didn't you tell me darling?" she cried, "You know you can stay with me".

"What about my sister? He said he would do things to her if I told anyone".

"Oh no he won't", I told her.

"Thank you so much for listening and believing me", she said as she hugged me goodbye.

We called a taxi and I promised the Nan that I would phone the mother, not the police. Frankly, I needed a strong drink, but refrained. I couldn't jeopardise my confrontation with the mother.

The phone rang, and she picked up. I didn't hold back, I threw it all at her.

"How dare you interfere in my family life", she screamed back at me. I was confounded.

"LISTEN! You either deal with me now at my house or I

will phone the police right this minute. You are living with a paedophile. It is out in the open. I will not let him have your daughter even though you choose to!"

I was totally disgusted when she sat in my home and sobbed that she suspected he had been up to things, but as he paid all the bills, gave them expensive holidays and was so respected in the orchestra she ignored her suspicions.

Her elder daughter never went back to live at home. She stayed with her grandmother and eventually I saw her grow up to be married.

The mother threw her husband out of their home and so the younger daughter grew up without him preying upon her.

I will never regret interfering. I am honoured and grateful she could trust and come to me.

61
Thyroid

A young woman came to see me. She was tiny, only about five feet tall, and very thin. She sat in my room looking small, scared and nervous.

"Try and calm down dear, please don't be scared of me".

I began her reading.

"You've nothing to worry about the children", I confidently stated about her four kids. "They are all clever and at least three of them will go to university. That's quite an achievement".

But the subject changed. "It's your husband I'm worried about". It was out of my mouth before I could stop it.

"Oh, he's okay now. He has seen a specialist and it's sorted".

"No, my dear, it's the throat area, thyroid and a cancer growth. He must have a second opinion and see another specialist

The colour drained from her face.

"This is not why I've come here".

This is not how it works; I don't know what I will tell people and cannot give answers on demand to trivial things like "Will I get the new BMW car?" "Can I get the expensive new kitchen?" Although the information I am given often seems insignificant at the time, ultimately spirits give me messages that are important.

The reason why she'd come to visit I pushed aside. The spirits were only interested in her husband's health.

I think the point was hitting home, the message was sinking in.

"So are you telling me my husband is ill?"

The spirit who was in my room was known to her - his name, the date he passed, the illness he had. This was where the news had come from, not from me conjuring up an illness. I felt sorry for her, but there must have been a reason why I said it.

She left for home.

She relayed the story back to her husband. He would have nothing of it. To be fair to him, you can understand why. He didn't know me, or I him. But his wife did not leave it. She arranged a private consultation with a top specialist.

The husband was diagnosed with thyroid cancer. He immediately went into hospital and had the tumour removed. He then underwent chemotherapy and was ill for quite some time.

He eventually made a full recovery and today is fit, well and happy.

His wife always said I saved his life, but I can't take the credit- it was the spirits, not me.

62
Stolen Ring

"I'm not sure if I should be here. I don't believe people like you can tell things".

"Oh dear, not another one", I thought to myself, whom no matter what I told, no matter how accurate, would be cynical and not believe me.

"Who recommended you?", I asked.

"Sylvia", I knew this lady she had been to see me for years.

"Look - I think this may be a waste of your time and mine. I think it's best if you go. I'm a very busy woman". I ushered the woman out of my house, then blurted out, "but just so you know, Sarah already knows about that diamond ring you are wearing".

The woman gasped and went very white.

"Oh my god. How do you know that?"

"Your mother, Sarah - she's here. She had a long, painful death with cancer".

"That's right. May I come back in please?" the woman asked.

I hadn't intended to coax her back in my house with what I had said, it was just something I had been compelled or made to say by the spirits. We sat down and began properly.

"Your mother says you stole the ring from the hospital and had the stone reset. The ring should have gone to your sister. The hospital paid out on the insurance and your sister, Rosalind, had a ring made but it did not have the same sentimental value as the original".

The woman looked taken aback.

"Are you going to tell the police?" she asked.

"Are you going to own up?" I answered back.

"I can't", she said.

"But you only wear it secretly when no-one else can recognise it don't you? Does it make you happy?"

"Can my mother forgive me?"

"Your mother is sad. Rosalind nursed her and did so much for her. That is why she wanted her to have her precious engagement ring

The woman was not happy that I had revealed so much. I knew she had no intention of giving her sister the ring, but I am not here to judge.

63
Reporter

A young man came to my door. He was very hesitant on the door step. He had an appointment, but he suddenly blurted out,

"I don't believe any of this! Most of you fortune tellers are charlatans!"

I needed this like a hole in the head.

"Why have you bothered to come then? I certainly don't need to see you", I replied tersely.

I started to close the door.

"Okay, well I suppose it wouldn't hurt if I came in. I'm a journalist and I'm looking for real proof that what you do is real".

I was still a little peeved by his attitude, but we went upstairs anyway. I looked into my ball. A large, dark grey car, a Volvo appeared. The area being shown to me was Kennington, South London and a man was slumped over the wheel. I then asked,

"Who's David?"

"In what context?" he said.

"He's someone close, about sixty five years old, suffering a massive heart attack".

"My father's name is David, but what's that got to do with you?"

He was testing my patience with his attitude, but I persevered.

"Spirits give me names, incidents, all sorts of information. I just say what I see, or hear. I can't decipher it".

"Kennington is not an area known to him or me. We don't go there".

A lady had appeared. Her spirit hovered above the young man. She said her name was Esther, she was David's mother and that she had died of a brain tumour.

"You are a con!" the young man shouted at me. "That's my grandmother. You must have found this out about me".

He had booked anonymously and considering he had almost not come in to see me, I would hardly have had the time to go looking for information about him.

I gave him a date which had come to me.

"This date will change your life".

"That's tomorrows date. This is rubbish. You haven't told me anything. I'm going".

He had hardly been in the room ten minutes, but I happily showed him out with relief.

Two days later there was a loud knocking at my door. It was 7pm and we had just finished our dinner.

Oh no, it was him again. He was totally different from before: subdued, almost sad.

"To what do I owe this visit?" my sarcasm blatant.

"May I please come in?" he asked politely.

I agreed to let him in, but before we had even reached the

top of the stairs he had started to blubber.

"My father died yesterday of a massive heart attack at the wheel of his grey Volvo. He was in Kennington

"Oh my dear. I am so sorry", I said.

"Did you make him die?"

"Oh no! No!" I answered. "It does not work like that. I don't have anything to do with people's destinies. God takes lives, not mediums. When I tried to tell you about your father's mother, your grandmother, she came through to us because she obviously knew his time was near. She probably came to meet him and receive his soul

It took quite a while for me to explain how a loved one would welcome and take care of a soul entering the spirit world. Esther must have made me see the Volvo and give details about David's heart attack. The Kennington area was a business meeting place for him.

It really is amazing how accurate the spirits can be with the messages they convey.

64
Ilford Palais

One of my most favourite places for giving readings was the Ilford Palais. After two psychic symposiums, which were both a tremendous success, they still had my name on their books and I was asked if I'd do my stint on Monday evenings. Whilst they played music, and youngsters enjoyed themselves dancing, I would be at the back of the hall giving readings. It was just a fun evening in aid of local kids in need. Children who suffered with cystic fibrosis, or were handicapped, there were so many that needed help.

It was my pleasure.

What young person can resist their fortune being told? My best crystal ball sat on its stand, reflecting all the dazzling lights of the disco.

My queue was enormous; it snaked right up to the front of the Palais. The kids danced and drank their drinks in the queue whilst the bouncers kept it in order.

I was amazed so many young men wanted to know how I saw spirits. They'd tell me what they thought they'd seen and if I thought the things they saw could have been spirits. So sweet!

The girls on the other hand, just wanted to know about their romances and love life. They never questioned me, they took everything I said as gospel.

I was often there until 2 or 3am until the large chauffeur driven car would drop me home.

Those were wonderful carefree evenings. I loved the music and I met loads of wonderful young people who over the years re-visited me and told me how I had influenced their lives.

One young lad worried me. He saw only the dark side of life and I knew he was suicidal. A breakthrough came - I found out he knew my son. I couldn't leave it. I persisted with him. He was a prefect at my son's school and knew the same lads.

"Please come and see me at home", I said.

The queue was getting fidgety. Readings were private and he'd had a longer reading than most. I cannot intrude, only offer help, but he stood out. Most of the kids were giggling and dancing, full of fun.

Two weeks went by. I did not mention meeting the lad at The Palais to my son; the reading had been private and confidential.

The next day the young lad was on my doorstep. Richard introduced him.

"He's from school. We're on the same project".

The boy smiled at me; neither of us mentioned the previous meeting.

"He's amazing at art, Mum. Show her your drawings while I sort mine out", Richard disappeared upstairs.

"You don't mind me coming?" the lad said.

"No, of course not. I'm glad you did", I replied.

He gave me an art book - not the project they were working on. It was picture after picture of graves, head stones, hanging men. Horrible! All done in heavy black charcoal. You couldn't fault the drawing. This lad had talent, but the pictures gave me the creeps. I did not need to be psychic to know he was going over the edge. He desperately needed help. I'm no doctor, but the services of a psychiatrist were required here and now.

I had to be careful. I slowly turned the pages of his "Private Book".

"I haven't shown this to anyone", he said.

"Would you like to talk this through? Describe the pictures?" I offered.

This worked. He started to tell me he wanted to die. Life, he thought, had no meaning, and he had no worth.

"You can stop right there!" I said "People would give their right arm to draw like you do. These pictures are clever. The meaning of them leaps out, they tell so much, a full story in pictures

This lad was straight A's in all subjects and had a confirmed place at Cambridge University. He was already so knowledgeable, but he was so intrigued about the spirit world.

"Ending your life yourself, is not on. You don't evolve. You'd be trapped between the worlds until you met with your natural time of death before you could move on", I stated.

He'd started to talk now, and couldn't stop. Two other boys had turned up on a motorbike and Richard was busy admiring it so nobody noticed our in-depth discussions.

"Thank you for talking to me", he said.

"That's fine", I answered. "Stay for something to eat. We're all going to have a barbeque in the garden later".

He visited often after that and the four boys won their project. Their hours of hard work spent in the shed at the bottom of our garden with drawing boards, a small fridge of fizzy drinks and portable television, paid off!

This lad left his dark life behind. He came through it all and is now happily married with two children.

Strangely and rather sadly I came in to contact with a family of a beautiful fourteen year old girl who did hang herself. I was shown her diaries after her death. The pictures she had drawn were weirdly similar to the lad's.

God only knows why they do it.

65
Teddy Bears' Picnic

I thought I would be a good idea to give the kids and the mums time out at a teddy bears' picnic as we were new to the village.

My front garden is huge, behind safe gates with enough space for games and an acting area. Peter made lots of child-size benches, to seat eight on each. I painted them all bright colours.

The trestle tables were all loaded with lots of tasty kids' food and drink, the whole garden flooded with balloons from every niche A young actress who was appearing in HARRY AND COSH on Channel Five came along with her friend to organize games and give the winning entrance ticket a giant bear, presented by George the publican at the Chequers pub.

For the whole day prizes, sweets and party food were free. I had been told by a local school Governor to cater for about two hundred children, but the dozens of hoops, skipping ropes, water pistols, along with balls skittles etc. were hardly used.

The nine kids and three mums who did come had a whale of a time and went home with goodies and presents.

The birds and local ducks were fed for days: obviously my psychic powers were not working that week!

No regrets - it was fun.

66

Strangeways Prison

Some of the scary phone calls I got over the years were from Strangeways Prison. God knows how they got my number, but after the first call they started to come in thick and fast.

Some of the men were quite polite, but there was always an edge to their voices; after all they weren't in prison for fun. Petty thieves, drug dealers and murderers were just some of the characters to contact me. Over the years I have had more than my share of being involved with murders, but this was a more sinister side. They were talking to me, telling me all sorts of grizzly details. I found it creepy and unnerving.

They would question me about what their nearest and dearest were up to on the outside. Were wives having affairs? What were their associates up to? I was completely out of my depth, their anger often directed at me. What was their future? When would I visit? Could they see me after sentencing was complete?

No! No! No! I did not want this. How had they found me in the first place? I'd tried to be kind, but it had to stop once and for all. I had my grandchildren to think of - supposing they tracked me down? Being talked at by lonely distressed prisoners who have committed dreadful crimes is far worse than seeing the spirit who could have been at their hands.

I contacted the governor of the prison. I'm not a councillor, and have no training in psychology, but I felt the situation I was in was dangerous.

"Could you tell me how they found me?" I asked the governor.

"We have open discussion for all prisoners. One day it was mediums, clairvoyants, fortune tellers and your name came up, and we had a discussion about you - who'd been to see you, who had heard of you, that sort of thing

This news to me was startling, but I insisted it must stop. I'm no snob, but how long could it be before one of the spirits came through and I offended one of the prisoners? The governor agreed to put a stop to it.

I did have the odd phone call from Wormwood Scrubs and Maidstone Prison, but that has all stopped now I have moved to my cottage.

67

Richard Beckinsale

The house I had lived in for most of my life was in Otley Drive, Gants Hill.

My family and I moved in the early '60s, followed by a young family either side.

Through out all the years, we never quarreled; we were all firm friends. If any of the kids were ill we did each others' shopping, always shared the school runs and, when the worst happened, the washing machine broke, we would help each other with the laundry.

How many days did we spend on days out in the school holidays?

The Greenline bus to Southend: days on the beach on a shoe string; we also did the train to Brighton, (much more expensive), swimming and picnics in the park. London Zoo, all the art galleries and museums. My children have seen the Mona Lisa, Constable's Hay Wain, Rubens and Leonardo Da Vinci etc., all of which I thought it important for them to see at a young age.

I was the instigator of a most successful silver jubilee street party, I hauled all my neighbours in to play their part.

Our next door neighbour was Dominique's teacher and

was chosen as our treasurer.

My very artistic son Richard painted a huge red, white and blue poster on wood. It must have been at least six foot by four foot and was erected in our front garden.

I made two enormous hats of red white and blue, again draped with Union Jack flags, plumes and streaming ribbons.

No one could have failed to notice Roxanne and me wearing our hats, collecting the money for the most amazing street party event we had all ever seen.

A six foot cake expertly decorated in flags, thousand of balloons ready to let loose in roped nets high above the road, (I never knew who or how they got them up there).

Five hundred people attended: every child received a china commemoration mug, along with a silver jubilee coin plus the usual sweets etc.

The road was blocked off with permission from the police, hundreds of long trestle tables and chairs were placed in the middle of the road, the bunting flags were strewn across every house, and I couldn't guess the electric bill from the hundreds of lights that flooded the streets.

After the street was cleared of tables the disco was in full swing for dancing.

The party did not stop until 5am, with not one complaint; a talking point for many months.

Several people approached me for a repeat, but it was surely a one-off; some things can't be repeated.

Several months later I came up with another idea - who would like a trip to the London palladium to see Tommy

Steel in panto? I organized two coaches, and they were filled in no time. We could only do two coaches because the tickets had all gone.

It was a happy drive through the back streets of London. The children were so excited - a panto such a thrill. We arrived very early, and it was suggested we split up and go for refreshments or to the shops.

I knew Hamleys toy store was near by so I went there with my little group. I let the kids loose; it was a wonderland stuffed with Christmas decorations and toys. I had warned them:

"DO NOT LEAVE THE STORE meet me by the main exit in 30 minutes".

I felt responsible, so I hovered by the exit. It was nice there - a huge train set was working on yards of track, with all types of trains, lights, tunnels and stations. It was magic, and with hardly anyone admiring it, I was happy. I turned left to follow the little train and, looking straight at me only one foot away, was Richard Beckinsale, the actor in 'Porridge' and 'Rising Damp'.

"Do you like trains too?" he asked. I nodded, but couldn't speak - very unusual for me!

He was really beautiful, with such a lovely smile and the gorgeous long hair so familiar in 'Rising Damp'.

My group were descending on me. Time was getting on to get back to the Palladium.

"Was that the man on 'telly?" I was asked,

"Did he talk to you?"

I had had the icing on the cake. The panto was magic

- we all had a marvellous outing; the music, scenery and acting thoroughly enjoyed.

19/03/1977, three months to the day, the very sad news was announced on T V that Richard Beckinsale had died of a heart attack. How strange he stood next to me on the day of the pantomime.

68
Otley Drive

Dominique was born in the house in Otley Drive. Roxanne left to arrive at the church in her wedding dress and several years later Dominique did the same. Seven of my grand children knew it as their second home, especially James and Victoria who I cared for when their mum worked. My garden was full of swings, a slide and a climbing frame.

I often did a children's party; one time we had seventy friends with their kids.

Then there were the endless relaxing BBQ's (weather permitting). My life was not all spirits: my family came first. Sadly, things change: the children had all moved into their respective homes. But my clients were still streaming to my house for readings.

Car space has always been a bone of contention in many lives.

I was getting many complaints from the new owner who had moved in two doors down.

If any one parked outside his house he thundered at my door. Three out of four times it was not a visitor for me; I'd warn people to park around the corner. Although I hadn't got a drive, I had the prettiest house in the street. A picket fence with gate surrounding the old fashioned wooden arch covered in sweetly smelling pink roses, lavender and clematis.

The wishing-well with water tumbling endlessly from the pump, and an old wooden bench, where my visitors could sit surrounded by rockeries flooded with flowers.

His frontage was a concrete slab. When he and his wife got married their large stretched cream car parked outside my house and the bride was photographed under my arch. I did not mind, it was a sort of compliment. All his visitors parked outside my house and when my husband came home from work in his large Volvo estate filled with his building tools he would have to park where he could; a very passive man, with never a cross word.

One evening Peter was at snooker when suddenly a large police van drew up and eight police officers got out. Six of them approached my door, and the other two went up his path.

I was kneeling in the front garden, weeding.

"We have a complaint about you", one policeman said.

"Hold on" said another "it's Shirley".

"Oh hello", I said

I'd recognized him as he came to me for readings: he was a black African gentleman.

"She's not racist", he stated. "I've known her and visited her with my family for four years".

My Jamaican neighbour had reported me, he said. Apparently I practiced voo-doo, I was racist and made his life a misery. He had started the war!

The police were very kind to me. and they told me he would be in trouble for wasting police time and if he upset me in any way to report him. News soon spread - I wasn't the only one he disliked. The Asian man who lived opposite him knocked on my door; he was over 6ft tall and told me if I had any trouble with the Jamaican to go over to him.

"He has made my life hell since he has moved in", he said.

A couple of weeks later I showed a lady in, as the first sitter left.

A little boy spirit followed us up. "We have a child here - he is only about three; he died of leukaemia". She started to sob.

At that moment my door bell was being rung incessantly, and accompanied by a hammering on my door. I knew who it was.

"Where have you parked?" I asked her. "Two doors down". "You'll have to move your car outside here", I said.

I opened the front door: I was ready for him.

His eyes were rolling around in his head, full of hate. His lip snarled and his fist was less than half an inch from my face.

"If you dare touch me, god help you!" I screamed "This lady's son has just died of leukaemia; please be kind to her".

He then started on her - she was a quivering mass. Curtains twitched, doors opened and a couple of neighbours tried to calm him down.

My lady couldn't move her car, she was shaking so much. The Asian man moved it and said he was a witness to this appalling disgraceful behavior. My lady's husband collected her, and said they'd get the car tomorrow.

None of us knows what is around the corner- the Jamaican's wife collapsed a couple of weeks later and after several tests in hospital was diagnosed with M .S. That was sad because she was nice. I put her in my healing book.

One evening I had an appointment with two young brothers, both 6ft.tall, very nice boys. We had only been in the little room 10 minutes when there was a god-almighty bang and screech: a car accident.

We raced down the stairs out to the front, where the sight was unbelievable. Two doors down the red Fiat belonging to the Jamaican neighbour was up his path in front of his door; the large Granada belonging to the Asian man was with it.

Thank god no one was hurt.

The Asian man had put his foot on the accelerator instead of the brake to avoid a dog, Dear god where was the dog?

"Dog, god where was the dog?" The two young men who were with me lifted the heavy car as though it were a toy. The Alsatian dog crept out unharmed, no blood, no limp and kissed its owner.

How very ironic, that had happened to his car, now he would be without it for some time.

My husband often gave his wife a lift –although not him.

He didn't change! He was one of my reasons to uproot and leave the house I had been in for almost forty years.

69

George

F ive doors down from where I lived was George. I can only describe him as odd. He was single, over sixty years old and had lived all his life with his aged parents, now passed.

He leered at you; all the other girls said so, not just me. All of us admitted we would hurry in or walk sharply away if we saw him. We were all young in our twenties with babies and young children: he never sought out the men, just us girls.

When we heard he'd hung himself from the rafters at home I suppose we all felt a little guilty. But it would have been difficult to befriend an elderly, strange man.

The two immediate neighbours had planned that if they did not like the look of prospective buyers they'd tell of George's hanging, but if it was a nice, young couple they approved of, they were to 'keep mum'.

A couple named Jill and Steve bought the house. They had their first baby, a girl, two years later, followed by a baby boy two years after that.

None of us mentioned anything about George, but when their little lad was about three years old, every single night he'd scream the street down with nightmares. We all heard it. Our bedroom was to the front of the house and their boy's room, although five doors away, was also in the front. I felt the child was seeing George. It was always 2am that the boy would wake up screaming, and George had died at 2am.

I asked Jill if he was okay.

"He's having nightmares. He says he sees a man".

How could I say anything? I could imagine her wanting to move house, yet I knew she loved the house and was very happy there. I decided to tell George, in no uncertain terms to leave. It was this family's home now. It was time for George to evolve.

At 1.45am, warmly clad with my torch and bible, I stood in their front garden. I called to George, spoke to George and even apologised to George for not being friendly when he was on the Earth plane. I told him I was shy, which, well, was not an absolute truth!!

It worked. He said he was ready to join his Mum and Dad but loved to look in on his old home because of the warm, family atmosphere, something that he had lacked in his own life.

The nightmares stopped and so did the screaming.

I did not tell anyone what I did. My husband thought I was out frog watching.

70
Pubs

I love to go into old pubs - not for the drinks, much more importantly for the atmosphere.

I had just spent one very hot Saturday afternoon dragging around every clothes shop in Wisbech with my daughter Roxanne, who wanted a complete new wardrobe for her holiday in the Algarve. I had patiently waited while she tried on every fashion and size in various shops. I didn't moan, kept silent and smiled, but I was tired, hot and beginning to get very fed up. My spirits lifted and I was immensely grateful when she suggested a cool shandy in the pub by Woolworths, 'The Rose and Crown'.

I was glad it was this pub as I'd never been in it before. It is very old and as we went through an arch into a cobbled courtyard it was almost like stepping back in time.

We were loaded with packages and bags galore. Toiletries, shoes, dresses - Roxanne was thrilled with all her purchases. She dumped the lot on a table and noticed how hot and tired I looked.

"Sit down Mum. I'll get you a nice cold drink", Roxanne told me as she went to the bar.

The pub was dusty, with cobwebs hanging from the high

ceilings and beams. I liked the place. It was cool inside, especially considering the searing June heat outside. Paint was peeling from doors and windows and I noticed the ceiling needed freshening up too. The heavy mahogany curved bar and tall stools were so in keeping with the shabby aged saloon, but there were hardly any punters in. At the far end was an old open brick fire place.

Standing next to the left of the inglenook was a spirit in a red coat-dress with high black boots and a white curled wig. I could also see two ladies dressed in old fashioned crinoline dresses, one pale blue, the other lavender. Both were wearing powdered wigs with curls piled high on their heads. A second red coat wafted through the thick wall, it was like a theatre act. Mist swirled around them.

I called to my daughter gesturing to the spirits.

"What are you pointing at Mum?" she asked confused, "I can't see anything. Oh, it must be some of the people you see".

The spirits lingered, totally oblivious of me or anyone else. It was very nice and rewarding to have witnessed their visit.

'The Rose and Crown' is a very old coaching pub; I could just imagine a coach collecting this foursome in the cobbled yard.

I haven't yet returned, but lots of sightings and phenomena have been reported about this local haunted pub that I enjoyed after all my Saturday shopping.

71
Two Rag Dolls

E venings of clairvoyance are hard work but usually very rewarding.

This one was for Imperial Cancer. The hall was extremely large, holding over a thousand people.

My first message took me to the last row at the back of the hall - the lady second from the end left side- A German pilot, Messerschmitt plane, he had passed in the war. The name Pieter was also being given.

"That is correct" the lady said.

Her clear voice rang out with a definite German accent. (I couldn't possibly have known she was German).

"He sends his love to Waltroud".

"Thank you - she is my sister", she said.

Oh, hold on, this spirit is coming to the front row to this gentleman here". I gestured to the front row.

"The lady you have just spoken to is my wife: we decided to sit apart because she always gets the messages", he said. We all laughed.

"Oh! there is one for you A lady who had stomach and bowel cancer - she's thanking you for all you did for her and sorting her effects; she is very pleased you were so thorough|. The cat is with her; she said you searched and searched for him, and he followed her to spirit two days after: he was run over.

"Thank you", he said. "The cat did worry me".

I continued with the evening.

I darted from person to person; the messages were coming thick and fast.

Middle hall back hall, front: I was getting a little hoarse. It was nearing a coffee break.

I'd do just one more before we took refreshments.

"There's a fire raging! "The spirit of a little girl is holding out a scorched rag doll; it is dressed as if from the little house on the prairie. Mop hat, flowered dress with white lace slip, edging showing, and white trimmed pinafore. She is taking me into a burnt-out totally wrecked house and she has stopped over at the Right side of the hall 1-2-3-4 5th row from the back.

"Yes you dear, the tall lady in red" I pointed to her!

"She is asking for Molly".

The lady in red crumpled up and howled - she was so distressed. I immediately stopped and closed for refreshment. The audience swarmed at me! It wasn't break time for me; everyone wanted my phone number. Answers to questions about their loved ones, and extensions to the messages I'd given them.

I escaped to a small room to sooth my throat with two cups of coffee.

A knock on the door the woman in charge of refreshments had brought the lady in the red coat to see me.

The spirit child had not left me, and I relayed the most haunting reading I have ever experienced in public!

"She was Sophie, your daughter Molly's best friend, and they both had identical dolls they loved, from whom they were inseparable".

"Yes".

"The house across the road to you, where Sophie and her whole family lived: they perished in a dreadful fire".

"Yes that's right".

"Molly says she sees her in spirit and I believe her", the mother said.

"Yes this is quite feasible; children are very psychic", I replied. "I'm so sorry I upset you".

"I wanted this, I hoped I'd hear from one of them; her mum was my friend".

"I borrowed this", she said. She had in her hand a rag doll.

It was the other doll! "Please may I show the audience and tell them - they will want to know that you could accept what I said".

It was a totally silent and awed audience that listened to me. I never know who I will see, or what I may say.

The German couple collected my phone number and visited me for many years at my home for private readings. Also Waltroud came to see me from Germany. On one visit I told her that she would move to a beautiful bungalow in Dorset.

They did in 2006, and have settled very happily. She was a wonderful lady; she taught German in a college. We still send Christmas cards to each other.

72

Richard - Eye Accident

The children were home it was school holidays. We were getting ready to go to London for a day out. Screams and giggling were coming from the front room: Richard was playing with a car booster game where a booster fired the cars in loops around a track.

Suddenly a god-almighty scream: he had put a biro pen in the booster, fired the trigger pointing at his face, and the biro was hanging out of his eye. I was shaking like a leaf and removed it.

The girls were screaming - he started to cry, and I was mad! Why the hell do boys have to do such daft stupid things? I was at my wit's end, and phoned for an ambulance.

It arrived quickly; they laid Richard down on the couch and the girls and I accompanied him to the hospital. The local hospital doctor saw him immediately and phoned the eye specialist at Old Church Hospital in Romford. We were transported again by ambulance to the specialist eye unit. After loads of tests, he was put in a small room and I was told his eye would have to be removed as it was so badly damaged.

He must stay quiet, and you must go home. 'Phone in

the morning and we will let you know when you can come. I was distraught; this could not be happening to my lovely boy. I 'phoned a taxi and we went home.

As I stepped from the cab a lady touched my arm. "Don't worry Shirley - life is not as black as you might think. Why are you looking so worried?"

I blurted it all out.

"Its too close to home", she said "Steady down and think, what would you do if it were someone else?"

"I'd put them in my healing book and concentrate on absent healing", I told her,

She took both of my hands: "You have done it for countless others, now do it for you!"

I thanked her; life didn't seem so black, there was a bright hope. I raced upstairs and put Richard in my book and prayed for him. The next day the hospital phoned me.

Mrs. Willcox we have some good news for you. Sorry we worried you yesterday - the eye will now not be removed, but it *is* damaged. Come in this afternoon.

Peter and I drove to the hospital; I left the girls with my neighbour.

He was in the next bed to a young man who had lost his sight in a car accident.

My son was cheering him up. After a consultation with the eye specialist they told us Richard would have to stay in hospital for at least a week.

Thank god Richard has his sight; only a slight scaring to that eye. I do believe in miracles.

73
Another Reporter

As a medium, you never know who is going to walk through your door. When I lived in London I would sometimes see ten people a day, and as I have always taken appointments anonymously I never knew who to expect.

One day a young man arrived at my door. He was very sharp and slick and I knew instantly he was a reporter. He was the boyfriend of a girl who had been coming to see me for many years, but he wasn't here to discover more about his relationship; he wanted to know about his career. He was extremely ambitious, and it didn't take me long to get into his reading.

I was seeing all sorts of things and knew immediately this young man was going to make a mark.

"The first thing I'm seeing is you writing for very major newspapers. You'll get front page stories and there'll be one front page story about a very famous footballer. I think the News of the World will feature your stories. It all seemed a little dramatic considering he had only been in my house five minutes and he wasn't a very accomplished or particularly successful journalist either, but it was what

I was seeing so I relayed it.

"What makes you say all this?" he asked. I could tell he thought I was a charlatan.

"Well, I don't tell lies", I told him, "and I only say what I see. There's no reason for me to make these things up. Do you carry around a camera?"

"No, I'm a journalist not a photographer". His ego seemed bruised at the suggestion that I may have confused the two.

"Yes, but may I suggest you buy one. I think it may come in useful to you at some point and help you back up your stories".

"I suppose so". He didn't look convinced by what I was saying at all.

We continued with the reading and I could see the relationship with the girl was not going to go anywhere, but he wasn't terribly keen to discuss his private life. I was very fond of her, but felt he didn't have room in his life for her and she would end up getting hurt. There was quite a sudden change of scene.

"Do you travel a lot?" I said.

"Of course. It's my job".

"Israel is standing out very clearly. I feel you are going on a holiday on your own, total relaxation for a week, maybe two. But you're not completely switching off. It's almost as if you are on the prowl for something. I'm seeing the 'Star of David', so I'm pretty sure it has to be Israel. There's a story there and I think it's to do with a woman: she's very wealthy and linked to the British government. I'm not being given any names, but it will be headline news".

He seemed deeply cynical at most of what I said, and eventually got up and left.

His girlfriend phoned me about a week after his visit. She told me how he thought I was fanciful and couldn't understand why she came to see me. She kindly defended me to him and said it was because everything I had said to her had come true.

Months later the young man made his name in Fleet Street. He had been out and about when he had seen a Premiership footballer and, as he was carrying a disposable camera, happened to gather the evidence he needed to back up his story. It made front page news.

Shortly after he turned up at my house.

"I didn't think there was a hope in hell what you had told me was true but it was. I wondered if you had anything else for me? If I hadn't had that camera I wouldn't have had that story. If we sit down and you concentrate maybe you can see what you get?"

I wasn't willing to entertain him. He hadn't shown me any respect previously and the way he was expecting me to just come out with information was not how things worked. I told him I wasn't prepared to do this and he left.

He made a huge splash in the news again with another story. It was as I had predicted and involved a female MP, and was to do with vast sums of money. It ran in the News of the World, and all other papers.

I'm not the sort of person who is against newspaper

reporters, I was upset about the lack of manners and attitude this man showed me, and I never did another reading for him again.

74
Welney

I t was late afternoon in November; not quite dusk. My husband as always was at the wheel, and we were driving through a village near to my home called Welney. The road was very straight and very dry, but either side of us there were fields and they were covered in water. They resembled a flood, but apparently they are always like this and nearby there is a huge swan reserve.

I looked out of the window and I was gazing across what seemed like marshland. Out of nowhere I saw two men walking across the boggy marshes. I knew straight away they were spirits as anyone else would sink immediately. It was strange. I felt a terrible chill run through my body.

"Why don't you drive a bit faster", I anxiously suggested to my husband.

"That's not like you. You don't usually like to go above 40mph", he said to me.

"I know, but I don't like this place. It's creepy He put his foot down. "Please go faster", I pleaded. I could see the two men walking closer to the road, getting nearer to us. I know to drive fast on a road, especially one surrounded by water, is irresponsible, but I just had to get away.

"You're so strange", my husband said.

It was now January and a gypsy lady came to see me for a reading. I had seen her before and she was very nice. She came in and we sat down and began to chat. For some reason I asked her if she knew Welney.

"How strange you asked me that", she said. "We just had a very nasty experience in that area".

"What do you mean?" I asked

"On New Years Eve my brother in law wanted to take his new 4x4 Range Rover out for a spin. He'd only got it a couple of weeks beforehand and the roads are nice and quiet out here so he decided to head in the direction of Welney.

He approached the bridge near Welney, when suddenly the car choked, spluttered and stopped. It was odd because he said he felt strange before it did this. Obviously he was really annoyed because this was a new car and it had let him down, so he opened the bonnet, checked this and that, pushed some buttons, but no joy.

Anyway, he got back in and thought he'd have a cigarette while he thought what to do. Before he lit up the car spun 180 degrees on its own! It literally was facing north then spun to face south!

My brother in law is a 6ft 4, hard-as-nails, man, but he leapt out and tore down the road. He was terrified. He ran to the nearest pub, but that was closed, so he found a public telephone and called his family. Four of them drove down there. When they got there they were asking him why on earth the car was facing the wrong way on that side of the road. Then one of them jumped in the car, turned the ignition and it started fine, no problems.

He tried to explain what he'd experienced, but was very shaken. Most of them said they had heard of weird things happening around there

"I had an odd experience when I was there too", I said, and I told her about the two men I had seen on the marshes.

"Don't you know what happened in that area?"

I didn't know. I hadn't seen any newspaper articles or heard anything, but apparently the story went that a long time ago the villagers murdered a man and buried him in the marsh. Another man from the village retaliated and he was chased along the marsh but then vanished. This all took place in November time. It all correlated with what I had seen, even the time of year I had seen it.

75
Simply *Sisters*

Two sisters came to my door. Only one had an appointment, but they both needed to hear what I had to say. I had seen them both before individually.

"Shirley, I want my sister here because I want her to hear what I think", one of the sisters said.

"Okay", I replied, "You know I tell it how it is; no flannel, even if it is hurtful?"

"Yes. We want the truth please", the sister stated.

"Your husband is seeing another woman and it's serious", I told her.

"Oh", she paused. "I guessed it, but I didn't want to accuse him or make a fuss and I know you think he is perfect", she said to her sister. "I've been checking up on him. Every time he'd go to his mate Tom's or Paul's or even his mother, I would phone with a silly excuse to ask him to bring home some aspirin or tell him I've dropped the milk and there won't be any for breakfast unless he gets some, and he was never where he said he was. I was always low key, no fuss, because I didn't want to arouse his suspicion".

We listened intently as she poured her heart out.

246

"I love him so much and thought we had a perfect marriage". She stopped for a moment, then from nowhere she asked, "Is the bitch a blonde?"

"No", I said. "She's small, petite and dark, just like you. But she is pregnant". Both girls gasped. I looked the sister straight in the eye and said, "And you know her".

The sister went bright red, then deathly white in a second. I knew it was her.

"I must go out to the car", she mumbled. "It's very hot in here and I need a drink".

"Oh no, don't leave. Your sister needs you. I have glasses and water here". I started to fill a glass for her; I wasn't going to allow her to slink off. I wanted her to witness the pain she was causing her sister.

"I so wanted a third baby", the wife said "but he always said two was enough. Our marriage must definitely be over if he's allowed her to get pregnant. He definitely won't allow an abortion, he's Catholic and doesn't believe in it. Slightly hypocritical, I thought to myself, to have such strong morals about one thing, yet clearly no scruples so far as sleeping with his wife's sister!

The wife started to sob and reached out to cling to her sister. The sister saw me glaring at her and dropped her gaze.

Shortly after they left.

About two years went by and the wife returned.

"Hello Shirley. I know you remember me!"

She was such a nice person, I could never understand why her husband left her.

"I know you knew it was my sister, you were sort of cold

with her. The whole family fell apart. My mother will never forgive her. My mum and dad always row about her. She was Dad's favourite and he insists she's our blood. My children never see him, they lost their dad. Her husband threw her out and kept the kids. So now it's just him and her and the baby living in a caravan

I saw this woman again about three years ago; she is now happily married to a splendid man and has a further two children.

This episode, however, was certainly not a fine example of sisterly love.

76
Tree Cottage

Many years ago my family and I went on holiday to Devon staying in a perfect, chocolate-box thatched cottage. It was beautiful. Outside was a huge oak tree and it reminded me, along with my grandchildren, of "Far Away Tree" in Enid Blyton's books: we would go and sit under it together and I would read them stories. Inside the cottage were two staircases that led from one side of the house to the other. The children found this enormously exciting, running back and forth and playing hide-and-seek in the various nooks and crannies.

There were six of us staying there: my married daughter who had bought her two children, my other daughter who was single at the time, and my husband and me. There was enough room for everyone to have their own space if they wanted it, and it looked set to be a nice relaxing little break, hopefully with good weather.

We had all selected our rooms and unpacked. At about 2am I sat up sharply. I could hear giggling. I figured the grandchildren were up and my daughter had taken them for a midnight snack or something. I didn't want to interfere, especially as the giggling sounded so happy. I listened to the children run across the landing and race down the staircase.

Next morning at breakfast we all sat down to a big fry up.

"I heard all that giggling in the night. Did you all have a midnight feast?" I enquired.

"What are you talking about?" my daughter asked me.

"I heard giggling. Didn't you take the children downstairs?"

"No. What are you on about?" my daughter looked puzzled and the children carried on tucking into their breakfasts.

The penny dropped and I realised that the children I'd heard were in fact spirits. This place was very haunted. Lots of things happened whilst we were there. The television came on by itself, cupboard doors swung open, pictures moved. I even set up a little experiment - I sprinkled talcum powder on the floor, placed an object in the middle of it, and then the next morning found the object moved and drag marks leading from where it had been. There was nothing scary about the house; it was too beautiful for that. It had an incredibly happy atmosphere, I assume because of its dominance of spirit children running all over it.

77

Mrs. Arnold

Over the years I have seen many people who have come to me for readings. Some come alone, some come in groups.

One evening there were three young ladies. We went up to my little room and I began, going through the various intricacies of their lives.

Very persistently a lady kept coming through. She said her name was Mrs Arnold. I asked the group if they knew her, but none of them seemed to know who she was. I described to them how she died. She was very worried about her daughter who was having pains in her head and kept mentioning Old Church Hospital.

Suddenly the penny dropped.

"I know who that is", said one of the ladies. "Don't you remember Mrs Arnold?" she asked looking at her friends.

"Oh yes! Gosh, I do actually. Her daughter is in Old Church Hospital at the moment", the friends replied.

No one knew exactly what was wrong, but the girl had been having persistent headaches and was having tests. It came out that she had three little children. Then the mother in spirit said to me that she suspected it was a brain tumour.

I repeated what I was hearing.

The girls gasped.

"I don't think anyone knows what's wrong with her", one of the girls said.

We carried on with their readings and the ladies left my house.

One of the girls phoned Mrs Arnold's daughter at the Old Church Hospital and told her that they had been to see me.

"Your mother came through", they told her, "and well, she told us she thought you had a brain tumour".

The girl was enormously upset, understandably. She didn't have a clue what was wrong with her, just that she was staying in the Neurological unit undergoing numerous tests.

Shortly after I got a 'phone call from her.

"I believe my mother came through to you and told you all about me", she said.

"Yes, that's correct. Have you ever had spirit healing before?" I asked her.

"No I haven't", she said.

"Would you allow me to come to the hospital and give you some?" I felt compelled to do this.

"Okay then", she said.

Old Church Hospital was some distance from me, so I had to ask my daughter to drive me there. My granddaughter Victoria was just a baby, but she came along with us too.

It was a hot, stuffy day, with no air when we arrived at the hospital. The hospital was very large and busy and we hadn't a clue where the Neurology department was. We circled the hospital several times trying to find the department. My daughter was getting angry.

"I'm fed up taking you on these stupid trips. What are you doing this time? And why on earth are we at a hospital?" she complained.

"Just leave me to it then if you don't want to be here", I said back.

A doctor must have heard us bickering and came over to us.

"Can I be of any help? Are you looking for something specifically?" he asked.

"Actually we're looking for the Neurology department", I told him.

"You're here. It's just up those stairs and through the door in front of you", he smiled.

I thanked him.

"I'll wait for you here then Mum", my daughter said.

I walked in and went up to the reception and asked for the lady, Alice, who I was to see. A few of the nurses knew why I was there; she must have told them about our 'phone call.

I looked over at her. She was sitting up in bed looking very pale. On the wall behind her bed were lots of pretty drawings obviously done by her children: paintings of 'Mummy we love you,' and 'Get well Mummy,' surrounding her. Her children were seven, five and three. I felt horribly guilty that I had told the girls who came to see me the message from her mother.

The doctor came over to me.

"Please be very careful with this lady. We know what you told her and you are right; she has a brain tumour", he confirmed.

I walked over to the bed and put my hands above her head. Sometimes you can feel enormous heat radiate out from the hands. I would never describe myself as a healer, but I believe any healer is an instrument used by a very strong force. It is almost as though I am the plug that goes into the wall and the power comes through me.

I stayed with her and we chatted. I felt she would get better. Eventually I left and went home with my daughter and we continued our day together.

I later heard that the lady left hospital. She didn't have to have surgery and was making wonderful progress and was getting better. There has got to be some sort of miracle at work 'out there'. I'm not for one second proclaiming it is me; maybe she was misdiagnosed? Who knows? I was just so happy and glad that she recovered.

78
Samantha (Circus)

One afternoon two young girls came to my house. They were standing on the doorstep looking very shaky and very scared.

"There's nothing to be afraid of", I told them, "in you come". They came in and made their way upstairs to my little room.

As they were walking up the stairs, I saw a spirit floating between them. It was a woman with beautiful, long chestnut-coloured hair. She hovered between them, looking free and happy. As we went in to the room I said,

"Take a seat girls, but I've got to say- we've got another girl with you All of a sudden I heard someone saying the name 'Samantha'. I looked at the girls. "Do you know a Samantha?"

One of them started to cry and the other was shaking.

"Don't be scared", I reassured them, "Nothing bad is going to happen

"She died yesterday", one of the girls whispered.

"But she looks wonderful", I said. "Let me see what else I can get".

She told me she had been suffering from bowel cancer.

She was only twenty two and had a young baby daughter she had left behind. Suddenly she looked terribly sad as she spoke about her daughter.

The two girls were sobbing and sobbing.

"Please don't worry", I reassured them, "She looks wonderful and she is saying she is free of pain now and is fine". As quickly as she appeared, suddenly she was gone.

The girls were still in pieces.

"Look, sit still, take a couple of minutes. I'll go and make some tea and coffee", I said.

I came back up and they were still mopping their eyes.

"I can't believe she came through so quickly. She only died yesterday. How has this happened?" the girl asked me.

"Well, this girl has obviously suffered very badly. She is now free from pain and wanted to talk to let you know that she's okay

We finished our talk about Samantha and I continued giving the girls their readings until it was time for them to leave.

It must have been several years later when I was sitting up in my little room, when out of nowhere I was picking up a telephone number. It was coming through to me over and over again very strongly. It was a local number to my area. I wrote it down and gazed at it. I went downstairs and looked though my address book to see if it belonged to anyone I knew. It did not match anything I had.

I went back upstairs to the room and sitting down,

I picked up the phone and dialled the number. It rang, then a very nice sounding woman answered.

"Please don't think I'm mad", I started, aware that what I was about to say was going to sound completely mad! "I'm a clairvoyant, and for some reason I've been given your number. While I'm speaking to you someone is telling me to say 'the circus, the circus, tell her about the circus'. It's got to mean something to you".

I'd said some outlandish things in my time, but 'phoning up complete strangers was a new one for me! I was expecting the phone to be slammed down at any moment.

"Yes it does. My granddaughter is five years old today and when her mother died she made us promise to take her daughter to the circus on her 5th birthday. My son is there with her now. My daughter was called Samantha".

I could not believe it. The same spirit who had visited me all those years ago had contacted me again. I was overwhelmed at how clever it all was.

Her mother was very cool and calm on the phone, considering how out-of-the-blue it had all been.

"I had no idea that this was your number. I see so many people, and it just came to me".

"When Samantha was five we took her to the circus and she insisted we do the same for her little girl".

As we spoke she said that they often felt Samantha's spirit around. They would talk to her and her daughter would go up to her picture, kiss it and have chats with her mummy. There was no doubt in their mind she was still very much present in their lives.

She thanked me for 'phoning her and as I replaced the receiver I felt thankful too. I felt such an idiot making that phone call, but I was so glad that I did.

79
Car Exhaust

One of the saddest readings I ever gave was when a young woman came to see me.

She was small, slim, frightened, with sad eyes and was clasping a photo in her lap.

"I don't want to show you the photo, but could you tell me something about it?" she said.

"I'll try", I answered, "but we have a young spirit here. He's a lovely lad, he only looks about nineteen or twenty. He's showing me a red car. This car must have been the pride of his life; there's not a bit of dirt on it, it's gleaming. But there is terrible sadness. I can see him in the car and there's a hose. I can smell car exhaust. That's the boy in the photo",

She began to cry.

"He's your son. He says, 'I'm so sorry mum.'"

I will never know what makes a young man drive to a lonely spot and do this. He had a beautiful car, a lovely job and nice girlfriend.

One day he came home from work.

"Mum I'm just going out for a spin in the car, I'll be back for dinner" he had told his Mum. "If my girlfriend 'phones tell her I'll be back later. Love you Mum".

Two hours later the police arrived at the house to say he had been found dead in his car.

I see an awful lot of parents whose children have done this sort of thing. It is so sad, but I don't know all the answers.

The boy's mother came to see me regularly over the years and in the end she found the strength to go on and rebuild her life, but I will never forget that time when he came through.

80
Murder (Mile End)

One evening three girls came to visit me. They were all sitting together laughing and giggling: this is usually because they are feeling nervous.

"Are you alright?" I asked.

"Yeah. I don't really fancy this, but my mate dragged me along", one of the girls said.

"Well, I'm coming to you first", I turned to the girl on my left. "You have a young blonde girl standing to the side of you and she keeps stroking your shoulder. This girl passed in a horrible way. She was murdered. I'm so sorry to say this, but I've got to. Her body was floating in a river. I'm being taken to East London, Stratford, Mile End; that way. This is horrible. She only looks about twenty".

"Please stop there. Stop!" the girl to my left cried. "This coat I'm wearing was hers. I bought it from her two weeks before she was murdered".

"She's agitated about you; your safety. I hope you're not walking alone down dark alleys", I said.

The two other girls suddenly piped up.

"We've told you not to do that! Why do you do it?" they said together.

"I'm not really afraid", she shrugged.

"But look what happened to your friend? She's asking you to be careful", I said.

The girl started to laugh nervously.

"I didn't like to tell you, but about two weeks ago I was walking home and a bloke tried to grab me down the alley", she explained sheepishly.

"What were you doing walking down a dark alleyway alone when the girl you know, whose coat you are wearing, was murdered? Why are you putting yourself at such risk?"

"She walks home alone late at night all the time. Strolls home at 1 or 2 in the morning", one of the girls said.

"Please promise me you won't do it again", was all I could say.

This spooked me: I remember the incident only too well! It took us back to a very cold December evening.

My younger daughter was going to meet her friend at Mile End Station - the trains met here from different junctions. It was a special night out at Epping Country Club; a Christmas 'do'.

"Why don't you phone Julie and tell her you'll meet her at the club; Dad will drive you there?"

"Oh mum! Stop it", she said "you always worry too much".

This time I was agitated even to the point of nagging "please don't go to Mile End - not tonight".

My daughter did make the phone call to her friend and her dad took her in the car. About 11.30 a news flash! Trouble at Mile End Station police with guns every where.

"Oh my god" I was calling to my husband "Look-Mile End Station".

What time did all that happen", he asked sharply.

They say lots of commotion and trouble at 8 o'clock this evening. Thank god you took her to Epping. I knew something was wrong".

My husband had gone deathly white.

"I'm so sorry, Dominique persuaded me to drop her at Mile End. Julie said you were stupid, and possessive, so Dominique planned to meet her there".

What could I do? An agonized wait for news of our daughter; neither of us went to bed. The sound of a taxi, and seeing her get out of it at 2.30am, was wonderful.

"Oh mum, I was so scared. Two policemen grabbed me and locked me in the ticket office with the staff - they didn't tell us what was happening, and then I was escorted to the Epping Club".

"The train Julie and the rest of the passengers were on was not allowed to stop at Mile End, so Julie and I met at the Club".

"Have you heard what went on? I had popped to the loo and when I emerged the station was deserted; that's when I was grabbed and marched off to the kiosk. The officer who drove me to the club was very kind, and when I told him who you were, and what you had said, he told me to listen very carefully in future to my mother!"

This was the evening a blonde girl the same age as my daughter was seen being abducted at the station. Two weeks later she was found floating face down in a river. It was the friend of one of my visitors. The one who used to own the black leather coat.

81
Circle (Rita Gould)

I joined a physic circle. For those of you who don't know, it's a gathering of like-minded folk who are interested in spirits, phenomena, and anything to do with the psychic world.

I was lucky enough to be taken as part of a group to go and see the very famous Direct Voice Medium Leslie Flint.

He lived in an extremely large house: a sort of mansion in Westbourne terrace in Paddington. The séances could last anything up to three hours. We would sit in a tiny cinema in his home, with a screen projector and a half moon of seats, just like the real thing only on a smaller scale.

Total blackout shutters, heavy curtains, then Leslie would go into a trance; if we were very lucky we could hear voices of sprits talking, shouting, laughing, just like we communicate.

It was strange and eerie but enormously exciting, as one by one the spirits would tell us who they were, what realm they were in, and how they passed, and tell us personal private things about our own lives.

Some of the spirit were extremely famous ones who had left the earth plane many years ago - Edith Cavel, Beatrix

Potter, Ellen Terry, Conan Doyle, Richard Burton, Isadora Duncan and ordinary souls: a man with a cart horse, army men from the trenches.

We were held in time in a different world - if only this exceptional gift was more common and available to more people: I haven't got this gift. On one of our visits Beatrix Potter came through.

Her voice was almost abrasive; very harsh. She talked of her little books she had written and her love of the Lake District.

This prompted me to visit the place which was her home. I often wondered about the connection with her, and my spirit photo I had taken at her home. It is the clearest photo I have ever seen of a spirit. All the séances were taped, and to this day I still have the voices.

Leslie moved to Hove, near Brighton, and as we were lucky enough to be invited we made the long journey there.

Sadly Leslie has passed over now, but I will be forever grateful for the 'phone call that would invite me to make up the numbers at a séance. This was when he was in Paddington; every séance was a magical experience and I count myself extremely lucky to have been given the chance to attend.

Another stroke of good fortune came in the name of Jack. He was one of the sitters in the circle I held on a Wednesday in my home. We had excellent séances – Jack's hobby was letter writing; his letters were like manuscripts. He was an elderly lonely widower and writing gave him life.

He found (god knows how) Rita Gould. She, like Leslie,

is a Direct Voice medium.

He corresponded with her for several weeks, and got four of us a place in her home séance.

These sittings are like gold-dust: harder to get than tea with the Queen. We set off for Leicestershire How exciting - away from home and responsibility for two days! The journey was fine for late spring. We arrived at Rita Gould's home.

Rita and her husband made us very welcome. We chatted about all that had happened in our circle and various experiences with spirits. They took us to the guest house where we were to stay the night, and after light refreshments we were taken to a lonely house right in the country - an ideal spot for a séance; quite eerie really.

The house was very old, with high ceilings, thick walls and large beams. Curtains were drawn at the shuttered bay windows, with a thick long curtain across the solid door. The room was in complete darkness but for a tiny red light.

The sitters were Rita, her husband and two of their friends plus us four. The room quickly filled with the smell of lilac, and a mist descended from the ceiling; this could be seen by the tiny glow from the still red light. The room was heavy with an atmosphere of marching soldiers, a Union Jack flag waved across the room and heavy boots were rasping on the bare floors.

My companions were gasping with astonishment at such activity. A bugle broke the silence blaring out a retreat. The room was suddenly empty, and whilst straining our eyes and ears for what was next, a Scottish woman's voice rang out.

She told us she was Helen Duncan, a very famous medium who was imprisoned by the government in the last war because it was thought she was a threat to British security.

She died when the police burst in on a public meeting when she was in a full trance at a Direct Voice séance (all this is in a book about her life) We all felt very honoured that she had visited our séance.

Conan Doyle and many other spirits visited. Once again I have the full séance on tape.

It was such a lot to take in I often think after the event we appreciate things so much more.

I have been extremely lucky and very privileged to have witnessed so much physic evidence. One instance of this being, towards the end of the séance, while we were all sitting quietly on large sofas and easy chairs, one by one we were touched by a hand. It was visible in the soft smoky light! Only a hand; no arm - it squeezed each of our hands, then moved on to the next sitter, unbelievable and very strange. For many years after, we marvelled at what had occurred: still I have not got a clue.

82

Sam, another exorcism

A medium friend did lots of exorcisms. One day a young girl phoned me: " Shirley you've got to help me; Leon is behaving very oddly".

"Ok" I said "Do you want to bring him round?" "Will he see me?"

I knew her and the family well; she was now in a relationship with Leon and had two lovely children.

A loud knock: "I'll wait outside", the girl said, and slid back into the car.

"Come in, go up", I told him, as he slowly deliberated; step, by step. "Take a seat. How are you"? I asked.

"I don't want to sit".

The tone of his voice was loud and eerie, and his large black eyes were staring straight at me, not blinking. He was a very black Jamaican, and the whites of his eyes were glistening brightly. I caught my breath - I was intensely terrified; his aura was mad.

I was frozen to the spot.

"Would you stand by the wall", I indicated. "The light from the window is too bright on you".

My voice was calm and soothing, a clever move on my

part; I had easier access to the door and my escape.

Suddenly he levitated: I was rooted to the spot.

This is the sort of phenomena we psychics crave, and here it was happening in front of me and I wanted to cry; I was frightened to death of him. The phone shrilled out, he floated down and for a fleeting second he looked almost normal.

It was Sue, outside on her mobile sitting in her car.

Thank god. "Phone this number now and ask him to come here, he is a good friend of mine - he does exorcisms. She rang off.

"Shirley I don't feel good, will you help me I'm really scared" - this coming form his lips; if only he knew.

"Leon do you have a grandmother who practices voodoo?"

"Yes she is very odd, I lived with her when I was young and my mother was afraid of her. Gran tried to get custody of me but my mother came to England. Dad was her only son, and he died, a strange story linked to his passing

"She used to send my mum effigies and she was terrified; she was always telling my mum to give me back to her. One of my aunts recently was visiting and she said my Nan would not be happy that I'd fathered half caste kids". (Sue is white).

The car was ready: "Leon we're going to see Sam, a friend of mine He will help you" I said.

"No, No, I'm not leaving here, I feel safe with you".

Oh God - he was looking very scary again.

"I will be with you and I won't leave you; I promise". I was speaking calmly.

Oh dear, my husband would be home soon for his dinner. Not a happy man if dinner was not on the table, but it would be worse if he saw the state of this man! My husband was always telling me to be careful after a nasty guy had almost attacked me in my own home. Fortunately my wonderful 6ft 4in son arrived home at the right moment and I was saved.

Someone up there does look after me.

"I must write a note to my husband", I was telling Leon, who'd gone off again.

With great difficulty I had to coax him down the stairs and into the car. He was holding on to my arm so tightly I had many bruises.

"Would you please accompany us, and will you be ok in the back with him Shirley?" Sam asked.

The twenty minute journey seemed like an hour; mediums do not have an easy life!

As we arrived Leon would not leave the car. I was half questioning if he should be in the care of a doctor or a psychiatric unit. He clung to me, fear was returning. Finally Sam and I persuaded him out and into the sanctuary.

It was like a doctor's surgery. Leon removed his shoes and finally released his grip on my now numb arm. We got him to lie on the black leather couch, and he finally started to relax.

Soothing music was playing in the background.

"Tell me all about him Shirley" asked Sam I quickly told him about his family and roots in Voodoo, "A witch doctor is here", I stated.

I felt glad he opposed the Gran! This was good to have such a strong spirit on our side.

I did admit my fear when he started to act so strange and levitated. Extraordinarily the levitation came again: I was very pleased Sam saw it; one person seeing it without a witness is a little hard to believe.

"This is the most troubled person I have ever seen", said Sam,

"Keep watch and tell me of every spirit you see leave his body There were at least a dozen".

We worked till 2am - both utterly exhausted.

"My son will take you home Shirley. I'll keep Leon here for the night", Sam said.

The exorcism worked. "Thank god, and Sam", I thought.

This is a very dangerous route to go down in the spiritualist movement; I wear a cross at all times.

Leon is totally recovered to this day.

Sam has now sadly passed to spirit.

I will never forget that experience.

83
Model (Rod Stewart)

I t never ceases to amaze me how many folk have walked up my path, and crossed my threshold; people from all walks of life.

I remember the tall American model: she had the most attractive southern accent and was dressed to kill. Why was she so well clad just for a reading with me?" I did ask,

"Are you going off for a modeling shoot?"

"Oh no, I always dress like this". She just exuded expense!

The reading was getting very interesting: she had just arrived in England after leaving the yacht of her former boyfriend, a Greek multi-millionaire. One of the air hostesses told her I would put her right: she needed direction; she was staying in the Hilton Hotel but was scared her ex. would cut off her expenses.

"Hope it doesn't happen before my dentist can give me a re-enamelling to all my teeth", she laughed.

(This of course was a Harley street dentist). Why oh why did they send them all to me?

She was a sweet girl - mid twenties, but hadn't got a clue about the world she moved in; hard ordinary work was not on the agenda!

"I need the company of expensive men". I smiled, yes - I had met her kind before. "I want fun, club life and music", she said.

I looked into my crystal ball.

"Go to London: make it a Thursday evening, and hang around this club - it is quite exclusive; lots of stars go there. You must look a little lost and helpless and I promise a man will sign you in- no strings but you're in. "The name Stewart is coming up - I believe he sings and has showbiz links".

She was not a prostitute, but not a 9 – 5 office girl either; just a model.

About two months later I was expecting a client. It was 11am; a nice bright sunny morning. The door bell rang on time. It was the American model, and outside my garden just off the pavement in his bright red convertible, was Rod Stewart, sunglasses on bright spiked blond hair, listening to music on his car radio.

"Look Shirley, you told me I'd meet him".

I had told her she'd meet a male, but I honestly hadn't a clue it would be him. She was ecstatic, and acted like she was already in love. The Ex was still paying her credit cards and the pearly teeth were fantastic.

If this is how the models fared I would book my next life to be one.

I saw her several times, and each time she came, it was in the red ,car music blaring. All my neighbours rushed out to get his autograph and I got four phone calls in half an hour to tell me he was there.

I didn't walk down the path to speak to him; the model was my visitor.

84
Gypsy (Natural Father)

It was a bright sunny Sunday morning Two sisters were coming; I had seen them before.

Totally different - chalk and cheese but very nice: the younger one breezed in; the other, elegant, smart, almost regal, followed.

"Shirley, it's happened just as you said!" the younger girl thrust out her left hand; a gorgeous diamond ring sparkled in the sun.

"We have already chosen our future home. It's brand new, four bedrooms, two bathrooms, and a cloakroom. My fiancé has paid the deposit, we have signed all the papers, I can't believe it's happening".

This lady was only nineteen years old, so it was an excellent start to their married life.

"Mum said I should come and see you to help sort the venue. Steve wants to get married in September, the house will be finished late June and there will still be enough time to furnish it".

"I take it the wedding will be the full works?" I asked.

The sister broke in, "her dress is stunning - she looks like Cinderella at the ball! Tony says he will feel like Prince

Charming walking her down the aisle".

Weddings in the family are such fun, and an acceptable boy for a treasured daughter is perfect. "Who is going first?" I asked, otherwise we would talk weddings for hours.

The bride to be.

I looked in my ball.

(This wasn't Tony - I knew him) A terrible commotion at the church.

"I thought Tony was giving you away?"

"He is".

"No it's not him you're with. Have you any uncles, tall, very dark almost black hair, wavy and long in a pony tail, Spanish type side burns and with an earring?"

"No uncles - only Mum and Dad; we've always called him Tony".

"Is Tony, well, healthy, fit?" "Yes - he's fine".

"Give me a minute". I looked hard into the ball.

"A gypsy woman with large earrings and bright silk clothes is holding out a silver horseshoe and a sheaf of white roses", I told them.

"The man I mentioned earlier is leading two horses with a white carriage. You are the bride in the carriage. Is this right - are you having a horse drawn carriage?"

"Yes it's my dream, that's what we are having". "Fantastic", I said.

The scene was rapidly changing: it looked like a gypsy encampment; the old fashioned Romany type horse-drawn caravan embossed at the side in silver, like the ones from the fairground. Small fires with large pots on tripods, children and dogs running around. The scene was vivid.

An old man appeared. He said he was the girls' natural granddad.

"What" they both exclaimed "You're wrong - we don't know what you're talking about".

The older sister was a nurse; she had just passed her sister qualifications.

"Shirley, you predicted I'd pass my exams, and yes, now I'm a sister!"

"You've never mentioned any of this before", said the younger one.

I took a long breath: "Tony is not your father! The gypsy man with the pony tail and earring is; he's father to you both. You will be re-united, and he is going to give you away at your wedding", I told the young one.

"Don't talk such rubbish, I'm sorry we came", the younger sister said

"Why have you said this Shirley?"

"You are implying Tony is not our father. This is serious - I wonder what mum and dad will have to say on the matter", the nurse said coldly.

I have said before, the words come out before I can stop them. We all felt uncomfortable. I certainly did not want to spoil the wedding! I'd seen these two lovely girls for a long time, with no hints of gypsy links before, but I could not change what I had seen.

The girls were gathering their things and the atmosphere was strained – spoilt after their enthusiastic arrival.

Sunday lunch was always special: today it was a delicious

leg of lamb cooked with rosemary and mint sauce along with roast potatoes and fresh vegetables. A lovely meal, but overshadowed by the expected phone call - had I opened a can of worms?

I was just washing up the last saucepan and the phone rang! The mum was screaming down the phone; my husband could hear her from the other side of the room. I'd never heard her swear before but now my ears were purple. I liked her, the mum, but "tone it, dear" I thought.

"You are admitting I told the truth, and the girls didn't know", I ventured.

"I'm coming round now I'm not going to leave it".

"But, but" I tried to say but the phone went dead. Oh dear - there goes my Sunday afternoon rest.

She was fuming - the car door slammed.

I opened my front door quickly before she could vent her anger on it! The mum and the two girls stomped up the stairs.

"This is something I've always dreaded – but fancy it being you who told them".

I stayed silent.

"That bastard has no right to these two girls; he has never acknowledged their existence. That pig beat me to a pulp- I was sixteen years old and got pregnant by him. I ran away from home to live with him, but was never accepted by his family because I was not one of them. You were three years old" - she gestured at the eldest daughter "and I was pregnant again. He was so cruel; he hit me all the time, and none of his family ever tried to stop him. I had black eyes, a split lip, swollen jaw and bruises all over my body.

My mother would have died had she known. I sent her birthday and Christmas cards and the odd photo of you, but I never ever 'phoned her because she would have known things weren't right and I wouldn't have been able to keep it from her".

"I hated him"

"They used to go out at night fishing and poaching".

"Our van was the first next to the dirt track. I was never included in the family meals so our van was not in the semi circle with the others, although he always had his meals with them! The only good thing about being placed there was it made my escape easy".

"It must have been about four am; I put you in the pushchair and we left - the dogs were all with the poaching party. It was freezing cold: the earth was so frozen I had to drag the pushchair for miles. Eventually I got to my mum's house, god only knows how I made it.

I was exhausted and passed out, and when I woke, I was in my own bedroom, warm and clean"

"Mum loved you on sight and to this day has never stopped spoiling you. My second pregnancy was difficult but with mum's love and care, you're here and we made it"

"Shirley! I didn't tell the girls all this; I wanted to tell them in front of you so they would know I was telling the truth" she said

"My big mouth", I uttered.

"I'm glad it's all out now. Tony lived next door I'd known him all my life, but never noticed him. He was four years older than me; smart, good job and lovely manners, and very good to his parents, but young girls always seem to fall for the rotters.

Gradually we'd talk; he would buy presents for you kids: he put a swing up in the garden,

and would often invite us for a day at the seaside in his car.

He was kind and gentle: I loved him - we got married and he was and is the best dad anyone could ever have".

I wasn't sure if I should be sorry I had spoken.

The bride found and made contact with her biological father and family, and allowed him to walk her down the aisle- the other sister shunned him.

85
Dick's Scaffolding

James my grandson was about four years old. His mum, my daughter, was at work. I was like all the Nans; I loved having him around - he was my little friend. Today was special: Grandad and his building partner were putting a new window frame in the large bay window upstairs.

The whole of the front of our house would be shrouded in scaffold.

After about their third coffee break the two men started to erect it. James and I were seated on a comfy sofa opposite the bay window down stairs, the television was at an angle so James could watch the workers. He so wanted to go outside but I said "NO".

The programme on the TV was his favourite, but he's a boy, and the men outside were much more interesting.

"Nanny look!" he was staring up the stairs "there is a man"

I quickly looked round; sure enough my father's spirit was looking down on us: he wasn't smiling - he looked very serious, Oh my god, the scaffolding! My father was the most awful worrier; he always saw danger! He had passed over long before James had been born, and he and

I were not ever close.

But here he was, warning us !

"Stay there James, darling. Nanny won't be long".

I went to the front door "Please be very careful - don't let the scaffold fall".

"Oh go in and mind your own business", my husband said. "Anyway, I'm off to B and Q - make coffee for us when I get back".

"Are you okay, Dick?" I asked. "Yes, I'm fine", he said.

James and I got back into viewing the programme. Then it happened: the whole scaffold covering the front fell, as if in slow motion. The noise was tremendous, and Dick fell from the top-most platform.

He was lying deathly still on the hard concrete path, with his head between a glass milk bottle and a rugged steel post; I'd asked my husband to remove it countless times. Dick didn't move at all. I 'phoned for an ambulance; it arrived in less than ten minutes, and the two paramedics started to tend to Dick as he re-gained consciousness! An inch either side and he would have been dead. They were trying to keep him still and telling him they must take him to hospital.

He was scrambling to get up and trying to move a heavy pole that must have crashed into his legs. I heard him say "I'm not going to hospital, no way".

"Oh Peter", I prayed, "please come home!"

The ambulance men were anxious "you need attention" We all knew that. "How on earth did he miss that spike and the milk bottle?" one said.

Dick was at his car door: "I'm going home", he said.

"You must sign this paper to say you refused hospital treatment, and we do not advise you to drive".

Dick scribbled his signature and drove off.

"What happened - did you see?"

"Yes - we were sitting here".

Poor little James had not moved from the sofa. Thank god I hadn't let him go out to watch. In need of a coffee, the two ambulance men joined me, and just at that moment my husband walked in "What you been up to now Dick……?"

We all stared at him in silence till little James piped up:

"Dick fell and made lots of noise".

"Oh god" said Peter as he went outside to look. He picked up the connection between two poles and it was loose
.

"Dick always puts up scaffolding like this", he said "he tightens it on the way down.

What happened to him?"

"He fell about 30ft, landed on his back, on solid concrete, his head only just between that spike and a milk bottle"

"How the hell did he miss them?"

"God Knows".

"You'd better remove that spike now! It's a horrible reminder of what nearly happened. I thought he was a goner - I'm really surprised he is alive", one man said.

"But where is he?" My husband asked

"He's driven off home".

"Oh god I'm going", Peter said as he left "I'm going to follow him".

Dick didn't leave his bed for six weeks, but now he is still as fit as ever, nearing eighty years old.

After James had gone home with his mum, I sorted out a photo of my father and put it among others I had in my little room. A few days later James was back again; he'd not mentioned the accident so I didn't.

The phone was ringing again. I was upstairs in the bathroom, while James my little friend who followed me every where was sitting on the landing.

"Ill get it!" he called

"Nanny, Nanny come in here nanny".

"Yes love I'll only be a minute, who is it?"

The phone was on the table but it wasn't the person on the phone who had caught his attention. It was the photo -"Look nanny; that is the man I saw on the stairs".

86
Orange Hair

I had a busy day ahead: the first two were due at ten.

Promptly they arrived. "We are mother and daughter", the older one said.

"Do you want to come in together" I asked. "Oh yes", she replied.

No one would have guessed their connection. The older lady was elegant, petite, with beautiful skin and colouring with my favourite hair style the French pleat, her soft silver hair curled in delicate tendrils framing her face. The daughter had bright orange hair, obviously dyed; her parting was black.

She had lovely huge brown limpid eyes, (her best feature) and a full mouth painted very bright red. I smiled; I did not miss a thing. I have been totally observant since I was tiny.

A once-over from me and I see every detail.

I looked at them both: the daughter had an infectious laugh - it was attractive and she was nervous.

Her mum was totally serene and composed. "Who wants to go first?" I asked.

"Let mum", the daughter said.

He came through at once - her husband, his passing

sudden, and he loved them both so much; no flaws here –
the happiest of marriages.

"You wear the ring all the time" he was saying "be careful".
She put out her left hand, where an enormous diamond
twinkled.

"He was always scared I'd get mugged, but it gives me so
much pleasure"

"Is his name William?"

"Yes", he says "you both travelled extensively and there is
nothing in the world he wouldn't give you, except the longed-
for child. You're adopted?" I questioned the daughter.

"Yes I am".

"William and I both adored her as our own, but he
always blamed himself that I never gave birth. After some of
the stories I have heard, I think I got the best bargain. No
one knows about the adoption, only us", she said.

"He had a stroke and slipped into a coma?"

"Yes that's right ".

"He loved to listen to you playing the piano".

"Yes he did!"

"He was the most wonderful husband anyone could
want; we had a perfect life", she said.

"How wonderful – it is so nice to hear this", I said. "Lots
of my friends have been to see you, Shirley, and said your
predictions were spot-on: what is going to happen to my
daughter?"

This young woman had travelled too, far and wide. She
had even worked in Hong Kong.

"I see horses, stables, the hunt!"

"Oh" they both said "go on!"

"Well, it is a very big house; sort of a mansion with extensive grounds. That's where the stables are, then there's a sort of ball room with high ceilings and chandeliers, a wide staircase that sweeps down into the ball room and, at the top of the stairs, there is a balcony landing.

Oh god, this isn't good: a child of about six years has fallen from the balcony and her spirit is still at that house; she was the daughter of one of the servants".

"I can't believe you can possibly know this" they were both agitated and excited.

"The man who now owns that house is my daughters new man friend and he only told us of the suspected haunting last week-end at dinner in Claridges".

"Right" they seemed to be moving in very expensive circles so my next outburst didn't seem too extraordinary.

"You will be given an engagement ring with a stone bigger than your mum's, a wedding, reception at the Savoy, and! He's a Count......" There - I'd said it.

Not an ordinary reading, and I did not even feel embarrassed.

"He is a count. There wasn't just us at Claridges for the meal: there were about forty people and lots of girls and women are after him", the mother said.

"I wouldn't lift a finger to get him", the daughter laughed

She was really nice - totally human, and what I liked was that neither of them were snobs. I told them a few more things and bade farewell. Was I getting fanciful; this was a bit way out.

Shirley, I told myself be careful you might be too old to keep this up.

My next person was a lady whose little girl came through; she had died of leukemia. Very sad, lots of evidence nothing way-out: I felt we were in a normality phase.

I had seen her before. She said that talking with me, and being told about things in the family, helped her. No-one knew her daughter talked to me.

About three months passed. One Wednesday I was out with my daughter and granddaughter. We were going to Marks and Spencer in Barking: I wanted to buy the children some clothes for our holiday that was looming.

I just love M & S children's clothes, and I selected a bundle. The girl at the till had been to see me for a reading, so had the one who was checking the sizes and removing the hangers.

"Oh Shirley I'm so glad it's you"

I turned my head; there was the lady with the French pleat, the one who had the daughter with the red hair.

"About the information you told us" (I sighed wishing the floor would swallow me up). "The Count and my daughter got married, the reception was at the Savoy, her ring is three times the size of mine and, they're living in the mansion".

"WHAT?" I stammered in disbelief.

I should not be so sceptical after all these years, but sometimes it is a little hard to take in.

87
Artist

An artist was in my room - he was weathered brown and his hair was covered in blonde streaks.

"Do you actually sail yourself?" I asked.

The scene I was looking at was precarious high seas and scorching sun.

"Sailing is my first love", he said

"Art - you are a natural; seascape, sunsets, storms, mountains; a total free spirit. I feel I should know - who is the young sporty handsome lad who died aged about sixteen years old with cancer?" I asked.

"He is my younger brother who went to Australia. You have also met my mother and sister".

I wasn't being told by a spirit who he was, I did see thousands of people. The scene changed.

"Do you have a dog? Small, brown and white; your brother's getting agitated - he says it's got rabies",

"No we haven't got one but Rabies is rife in Casablanca - that's my home".

"£40,000 a nice amount of money: have you recently handled this sum?"

"No but it would be nice!"

"Who is Francesca?" I asked

"My better half".

"Have you done a lot of sailing" I asked, "because there are lots of boats; not in a harbour, but separately, sailing on the ocean".

"I know what you're seeing! I collect boats at various ports all over the world and deliver them to whoever buys them. It's a fantastic opportunity for me and lots of money in it. I was in the navy for many years".

"What made you pick Casablanca?" I asked

"It's paradise, and very cheap. I love the climate; it's wonderful, suits me to a tee. My girlfriend's there, I paint, and with my ocean trips we have a marvellous life.

Who else do you know who sails exotic expensive boats for millionaires and gets paid for it?" he asked me.

I saw the spirit of his brother: he gave up a lot of family facts and was gone.

"You have a son, he tells me, and the boy is the image of him".

"Yes, he was the living image, but I've not seem him in twenty years".

"But your brother says the boy would love a reunion; he talks of you, as if you're in his life".

"None of my family has had contact" he said "except the brother in spirit!"

I said "that's the advantage - the spirits know everything. When are you sailing?"

"Day after tomorrow", he said, eyes glazing. "It would be nice. I've always imagined giving him a bear hug. My mother has never encouraged it; she totally disliked the boys' mum, and we never married. Looking back, my mother did interfere almost to the point of driving her away. Mother said it wouldn't be fair to her, or the boy, with me at sea, so she took off".

"You still have tomorrow: do it for your brother; he wants this, do it for him".

About a month later I had a phone call; it was the artist.

"Shirley thank you, I found my son!"

"He is the image of me - my brother and I were like twins. He's coming to visit here! His mother has moved on, married with two girls. She was nice and polite and so was her husband; they don't object to the reunion with my son. Oh, and you'll never guess,

Francesca took in a small brown and white dog. He started acting strangely and, because I'd phoned and told her you mentioned rabies, she called in the vet. The dog did have early stages of rabies - they told her she was very lucky".

"The other bit of fantastic news: £40,000 was waiting for me on the sale of three paintings I'd done for a large hotel, as they had helped to advertise the area. Thank you so much - I'll visit next time I'm in England".

88
Spirit

The kids were at school, and I had the day to myself. I thought I'd start with the washing.

The machine had finished its first run, there was a good wind and the sun was warm. "I'll do the nets and clean the windows".

A loud shout! Someone called my name; it came from the house again:

"Shirley!"

I went in cautiously; the street door was locked - I always slipped the bolt when in alone.

"What the hell.... "

There was a freezing draught, yet in the garden it was hot. I slowly mounted the stairs to go into my little room! I felt spooked, but the atmosphere here was good. I crossed to the window: an ambulance was across the road and two ambulance men were carrying out a stretcher; on it was my nice friendly neighbour who I had known for twenty-odd years.

He was lying still, not covered by a sheet - but I felt he was dead.

Before they took him into the ambulance and out of

sight, I watched his spirit leave his body: a sort of mist of ectoplasm wafted around him, and he rose out of his body and drifted upwards.

The spirit, an exact replica of the body, had floated upwards. The ambulance man covered him with a sheet! He had gone. They escorted the wife back indoors, closed the doors of the ambulance and drove off.

"Who had called my name twice?

I'm glad I witnessed this; I saw another spirit leave a body when I had my appendix out and was convalescing in hospital.

Another occasion: very similar - door locked, hanging out the washing, when a voice called me.

Not imagination; a voice from inside the house while I was in the garden. As soon as I went inside the phone rang. A voice said:

"Shirley, Mick's dead! He just fell on the floor this morning; at first I thought he'd tripped over, but he just crumpled in front of me. The doctor has just left - I called an ambulance and they have taken him away. The doctor told me I shouldn't be alone, so I thought of you. Can I come around? Would you phone his mum for me?"

"Yes of course, come now", I said "see you soon". "Thank you - I'll get a taxi".

I was in shock, but no wonder she sounded so strange: it hadn't hit home yet. What a tragedy - he was only thirty five; a wonderful guy, with perfect manners, and a good person. His mum and dad would be in bits; they had gone on their first exotic cruise. His wife would find it so very hard: the poor love, she was expecting their first baby as I had predicted.

So very unfair - he wanted to be a dad.

Another destiny!

89
Three Shirleys

A young woman often came to see me. Her name was Shirley too.

She had a wonderful personality, and she was also very psychic. We always ended up screaming with laughter at what happened to either of us.

It was a Thursday evening, about ten past seven. We were going over all her personal life - kids, man troubles etc. She was young enough to be my daughter, and I was very fond of her.

She was a tough, private person,

"You always know exactly what he is up to, Shirley" she told me, "and you are the only one I let close enough to know everything".

The scene changed - it was awful: I could see the spirit of a young fit man who had hanged himself. It looked as if he was enclosed by bars, like a prison. He pointed at the clock - just seven thirty p m. He said his name was Don.

"Shirley you know him".

"Oh my god" I said "he's just done it!" Seven thirty on the dot.

"Who do you know in prison named Don? He looks

about twenty three to twenty five; a nice-looking boy, mousey fair hair. The East Ham area is being given".

Shirley had gone deathly white and was shaking badly.

"Will I see him, will he follow me?"

"I do know who he is. I've known the whole family most of my life; we were at school together. Never boyfriend and girlfriend, but he was a laugh and fun".

"But Shirl, he changed. He did two horrendous murders: an old couple".

She told me all the detail; it was horrific, and I stopped her. The old couple's son, had been here to see me. Some things in life you hear and never forget. The son was a policeman.

"Shirley I feel bad, have you got any booze?" she asked.

"Yes - brandy, gin what would you like?" I said.

"Anything - I'm not driving; I'm too scared. I'll get a taxi home".

We both had a brandy, Shirley started to sob.

"He terrified me. He was a thug, and I can't think why he came through to me? He was always in pub fights. A member of a vicious gang; every one steered well away.

One guy got his knee caps broken and there were questions over several stabbings.

"Would you feel better if I gave you my spare cross it's nice, gold, and I have worn it in churches", I offered.

"I'll borrow it until I buy one", she replied.

"No - I've always planned to give it to someone who needs it", I said, as I fastened it around her neck.

"Don is saying he couldn't live with what he had done

any longer, and he is truly sorry for what he did and doesn't deserve to live any more".

"Shirley he wants you to tell his mother he is sorry for everything, Could you do this?"

"Yes I'm feeling a bit better now" she said "'I'll call in on my way home".

I made her a coffee with a little more brandy in, called her a cab, and she was gone.

I felt uneasy; when the son came here, his two elderly parents came through. I hope I will never see such brutality ever in my life again.

And here was the spirit who had done this.

A frightfully uneasy coincidence: Don's mother found her way to my door. It wasn't her who had done this awful crime; she was my age, another Shirley.

Three Shirleys, all in shock, linked to a man that had just hanged himself.

90
Madam

A young mum: vivacious, petite, blonde, with two lovely daughters.

Single and just managing - it must be very difficult bringing up kids on your own.

The house has to be warm in winter, the rent or mortgage has to be paid or the tenant can be thrown out. Then there are the countless bills; clothing food and transport. No wonder ladies take jobs convenient to their needs.

This one was a receptionist in a sauna - perhaps another name for a brothel.

She was not a prostitute; she had been to me for several readings! "Be very careful - I'm seeing a police raid", I said "and you are in court, a hefty fine".

"I don't think so, Shirley, I'm only answering the 'phone and doing the bookings".

About three months later I read in the newspaper SAUNA RAIDED BY POLICE-MADAM FINED IN COURT.

Oh my god! I read it through: yes, it was her, named and shamed. The so-called police evidence said she was prosecuted because she arranged appointments for the pubic to see prostitutes. I wasn't worried about the hefty fine, someone would look after her.

She phoned that evening

"Shirley you were right, did you hear about the raid?"

"Yes, I saw it in the papers today".

"Guess what, the judge who fined me was one of our regulars; while he was reading the riot act to me his eyes were twinkling, I was smiling, he paid my fine".

We both laughed.

"Shirley can you fit me in for a reading soon. I need a change, please help me".

She came two weeks later!

"Have you anyone in Canada? Relatives, friends I'm seeing you go there – there's thick snow, and it's freezing cold".

"My mother lives there now. I was hoping to go for Christmas and New Year".

"Yes, all three of you, it will be perfect. Hold on, I'm so sorry I'm seeing a fire", I said. "What is going on here?"

"Is it a plane, a car?" she asked

"No, a home. I'm not sure where it is but it's a total burn-out".

As no more information appeared we carried on from where we had left off.

"What about a job? I can't go back to the sauna even though it was a fun job".

"Have you ever done hairdressing", I asked.

"Yes I used to be a stylist but I don't want to work on Saturdays

"You will be in Canada for at least three weeks. It's late November now; hardly time to settle at a job before your holiday. Why don't you do some casual shop work? Something new here: next year a brand new romance. He looks very nice, do you know a Tom?"

"No, but you're usually right".

"Canada is not definite Shirley; we can only go if my mother can have us".

"She will", I said "A very happy Christmas and New Year is on the cards". Then she left.

Two weeks later, a phone call.

"Guess what Shirley - Mum has sent five hundred pounds towards our fare: she had an insurance policy mature and our plane tickets are booked; we are off to Canada".

"I'm so pleased. Have a wonderful time", I said.

During their return journey tragedy had struck; their beautiful chalet bungalow home had burnt to the ground with all their possessions.

This was so unfair; such a lovely girl - she wouldn't do harm to anyone. They moved into rented property whilst their insurance company investigated the fire and re- build, and the assessors went to town on the contents claim.

It was New Year and I felt her luck would change; if anyone deserved luck it was her.

A friend of hers was giving her a cheering-up party. Lots of friends had raided their cupboards for old group photos of her and the kids, and any party photo pictures where her two had attended. It was so heart-breaking; their entire photo collection had been destroyed. It was truly amazing what her friends had sorted between them, and a bulging photo album was given to her.

She cried and cried

The guy, a friend of one of the girls, had put it together, He was a wiz with photos, and his name was TOM! Is this a coincidence?

If her house had not burnt down she would not have needed the photos and would not have met Tom.

To cut a long story short, they married and are still blissfully happy.

91
Billy - Holborn

I suppose I've always seen more women than men; ladies are more into relationships, but today it was a man.

He had only been in my room for two minutes and a spirit lad came through. He was about twenty years old and said his name was "Billy".

The man looked at me sharply. "What is he saying?"

"Nothing yet", I replied. "Until he shows me where he is and how he passed I cannot say, except he is deeply disturbed. "Did you know he was into the occult?"

"Not exactly", he said.

I waited and watched; this was unnerving. I did not understand exactly what he was mixed up in - I had never come across this before.

The lad was obviously highly intelligent but had been taking drugs. I'm not sure if it was the occult link or the drugs or even both, but this lad was very unbalanced at the time of his death.

"He wanted to fly, but not in a plane", I said. I was trying to be gentle with the man.

"This lad is somewhere in the London area". The man nodded, He knew.

I was getting flashes of London, the Holborn area in particular. Billy took off from an enormous height attempting to fly.........and died.

"It was awful, such a waste of a beautiful person", I told the man.

He took me to the grave. His dad was quiet. "We were never close, I couldn't reach him", he said. "But he had lots of friends; about five hundred came to the funeral"

"The spirit is very calm and at peace", I told him, "no one could possibly guess at the reason behind this passing".

The father was searching for the truth but I had no further messages from Billy. The fact that he came through to his dad was good, however brief. Some spirits give many many details and others give us few, so we must be grateful for any contact at all.

The father had come up from Brighton to see me. This was his only child and he and his wife were separated.

"I'm going to his grave now", he said. I felt very sorry for him but if a spirit only stays for a brief period there is nothing that I can do.

92
The End

I have seen spirits all my life from as young as the age of six.

I count my self enormously lucky to have met so many people linked to the spiritualist movement with extraordinary gifts.

Doris Stokes an old favourite
Gordon Higginson's materialization at Stanstead Hall
Leslie Flint's Direct Voice
Rita Gould, also Direct Voice, Doris Collins
Eileen Roberts – who gave me wonderful advice, when I appeared at the Quaker Hall in Romford.

The outstanding Phenomena as Helen Duncan spoke:

Conan Doyle
Beatrix Potter
Ellen Terry
Edith Cavil

And countless others at direct voice séances.

I have levitated and also seen another person achieve this.

Witnessed our table rise and turn, received direct voice in my home.

Out of body experiences – floating above one's own body whilst seeing your self below. The first time this happened I was only seventeen; I was terrified I would not get back into my body; as you now all know I did.

To be continued.